409680

D1331575

COOL
AMSTERDAM
LIFESTYLE

teNeues

PRICE CATEGORY

$ = BUDGET $$ = AFFORDABLE $$$ = MODERATE $$$$ = LUXURY

COOL
CONTENT

INTRO

914.
92
COO

"I AM-STERDAM." OF COURSE THE DUTCH CAPITAL FEATURES UNMISTAKABLE CANALS WITH THEIR MANSIONS AND FAMOUS MUSEUMS WITH MAGNIFICENT VAN GOGHS, REMBRANDTS, AND VERMEERS. BUT AMSTERDAM CAPTURES VISITORS PRIMARILY WITH ITS SOUL: TOLERANT, CASUAL, BOLD, AND SOMETIMES A LITTLE CRAZY. IT IS A CITY THAT LOVES TO EXPERIMENT. NEW DISTRICTS WITH AVANT-GARDE ARCHITECTURE HAVE EMERGED ALONG THE WATER. TRENDY RESTAURANTS AND STYLIZED LOUNGES HAVE MOVED INTO COOL INDUSTRIAL COMPLEXES IN THE OLD HARBOR AREA. MUSEUMS HAVE BEEN GIVEN A MAKEOVER. SHOPS PRESENT INNOVATIVE DUTCH DESIGN. EVER CHANGING, AMSTERDAM IS ALWAYS SURPRISING.

„I AM-STERDAM". NATÜRLICH GIBT ES IN DER NIEDERLÄNDISCHEN HAUPTSTADT DIE UNVERWECHSELBAREN GRACHTEN MIT IHREN HERRENHÄUSERN UND DIE RENOMMIERTEN MUSEEN MIT SEHENS-WERTEN VAN GOGHS, REMBRANDTS UND VERMEERS. ABER AMSTERDAM EROBERT DIE BESUCHER VOR ALLEM MIT SEINER SEELE: TOLERANT, LÄSSIG, FRECH UND MANCHMAL ETWAS VERRÜCKT. EINE STADT MIT LUST AM EXPERIMENT. AM WASSER SIND NEUE VIERTEL MIT AVANTGARDISTISCHER ARCHITEKTUR ENTSTANDEN. TRENDIGE RESTAURANTS UND GESTYLTE LOUNGES SIND IN COOLE INDUSTRIEKOMPLEXE IM ALTEN HAFENGEBIET EINGEZOGEN. MUSEEN HABEN EINEN NEUEN LOOK BEKOMMEN. SHOPS PRÄSENTIEREN INNOVATIVES DUTCH DESIGN. AMSTERDAM IST IM WANDEL UND ÜBERRASCHT.

HOTELS

ESTHERÉA

Singel 303–309 // Centrum
Tel.: +31 (0)20 6 24 51 46
www.estherea.nl

Tram 1, 2, 3 Spui

Prices: $$$$

MAP N°

This jewel is located in a row of canal houses from the 17th century.
Hotel Estheréa is an elegant family hotel, furnished with wool carpets,
crystal chandeliers, designer wallpaper, and classic furniture. Colors,
shapes, and materials all blend together harmoniously. The library and
the breakfast room are as cozy as a living room. From the lounge, you
can gaze out over the houseboats moored along the idyllic Singel canal.

Dieses Juwel befindet sich in einer Reihe zusammengefügter Grachten-
häuser aus dem 17. Jahrhundert. Das Estheréa ist ein Familienhotel im
eleganten Stil, ausgestattet mit klassischen Möbeln, Wollteppichen,
Kristallleuchtern und Designertapeten. Farben, Formen und Materialien
harmonieren wunderbar. Heimelig wie das eigene Wohnzimmer sind die
Bibliothek und der Frühstücksraum. Von der Lounge schweift der Blick
über die idyllische Singel mit Hausbooten.

13

Weteringschans 136 // Centrum
Tel.: +31 (0)20 6 62 32 33
www.hotelv.nl

Tram 4, 7, 10, 25 Frederiksplein

Prices: $$

Located on the edge of the trendy De Pijp district, Hotel V is pleasant
and uncomplicated. With its large, freestanding fireplace, curving sofa,
and relaxed atmosphere, the lobby immediately makes guests feel at
home. The style is retro, featuring warm brown tones, leather and
wood, globe lamps and furniture classics. This design is carried through
to the rooms as well. Hotel V stands for "Revival of the Seventies," but
with 21st century comfort.

Sympathisch und unkompliziert ist dieses Haus am Rande des Szene-
viertels De Pijp. Durch den großen, frei stehenden Kamin mit halbrundem
Loungesofa in der Lobby und die entspannte Atmosphäre fühlt der
Gast sich sofort zu Hause. Der Stil ist retro mit warmen Brauntönen,
Leder und Holz, Kugellampen und Möbelklassikern. Das Design ist
konsequent bis in die Zimmer durchgeführt. Hotel V steht für „Revival
of the Seventies", aber mit dem Komfort des 21. Jahrhunderts.

PULITZER

Prinsengracht 315-331 // Centrum
Tel.: +31 (0)20 5 23 52 35
www.hotelpulitzeramsterdam.nl

Tram 13, 14, 17 Westermarkt

Prices: $$$$

Several restored canal houses from the 17th and 18th century were combined to create this five-star hotel. Inside and out, this luxury hotel on Prinsengracht and Keizersgracht canals wins guests over with its comfortable historic ambience paired with modern amenities. Guests can choose from rooms with a view of the idyllic canals or rooms that look out upon the peaceful garden in the interior courtyard. And if you need respite from the city's hectic pace, you can relax in the garden café.

Für das Fünf-Sterne-Hotel wurden mehrere restaurierte Grachten-häuser aus dem 17. und 18. Jahrhundert zusammengefügt. Sowohl außen wie auch innen überzeugt das Luxushotel an der Prinsen- und der Keizersgracht. Es bietet Komfort in historischem Ambiente und alle Annehmlichkeiten der heutigen Zeit. Zur Auswahl stehen Zimmer mit Blick auf die idyllischen Grachten oder auf den ruhigen Garten im Innen-hof. Und wem die Hektik der Großstadt zu viel wird, der entspannt im Gartencafé.

Prinsengracht 717 // Centrum
Tel.: +31 (0)20 4 27 07 17
www.717hotel.nl

Tram 1, 2, 5 Prinsengracht

Prices: $$$$

The house number is also the name: The address at Prinsengracht 717 stands for a first-class, privately owned hotel in a monumental mansion. This comfortable hotel has just nine rooms and suites, each with its own character and furnished with loving details. Guests are received in a cozy salon like a friend of the family. In the afternoons, coffee, tea, and cake are served on the shady patio, while in the evenings guests can enjoy a glass of house wine—who would ever want to leave?

Die Hausnummer ist gleichzeitig der Name: Die Adresse an der Prinsengracht 717 steht für ein erstklassiges, privat geführtes Hotel in einem monumentalen Herrenhaus. Nur neun Suiten und Zimmer hat das behagliche Hotel. Jedes hat seinen eigenen Charakter und ist mit liebevollen Details eingerichtet. Wie ein Freund des Hauses wird der Gast in einem gemütlichen Salon empfangen. Nachmittags werden im schattigen Patio Kaffee, Tee und Kuchen serviert, abends gibt es noch ein Gläschen Hauswein – wer will da noch abreisen?

THE GRAND

Oudezijds Voorburgwal 197
Centrum
Tel.: +31 (0)20 5 55 31 11
www.sofitel-legend-thegrand.com/
amsterdam

Tram 4, 9, 14, 16, 24, 25 Spui

Prices: $$$$

MAP N° 5

The first and only Sofitel Legend hotel in Europe to date, this five-star hotel is located in a building in the heart of old Amsterdam, steeped in history. The hotel's services include butler service as well as a guided hotel tour in which guests can learn about the history of the house. Stylish rooms and suites offer ultimate comfort, and most feature a view of the canal. The restaurant is considered to be one of the best in the city.

Europas erstes und bis jetzt einziges Sofitel-Legend-Hotel. Das Fünf-Sterne-Hotel liegt mitten in der Amsterdamer Altstadt und ist in einem geschichtsträchtigen Gebäude untergebracht. Der Butlerservice gehört genauso zu den Leistungen wie ein geführter Hotelrundgang, bei dem man über die Geschichte des Hauses informiert wird. Die stilvollen Suiten und Zimmer bieten Komfort auf höchstem Niveau, meist mit Grachtenblick. Dazu gilt das Restaurant als eines der besten der Stadt.

Behind the façade of this listed bottle gable house, guests are surprised by a modern yet cozy atmosphere. This small, personal hotel features contemporary furnishings and a first-class location on the Herengracht canal. Rooms are decorated in peaceful warm tones, and XXL-sized reproductions of Old Dutch masters hang on the walls. Shops, restaurants, and clubs are all within easy walking distance.

THE TIMES HOTEL

Herengracht 135–137 // Centrum
Tel.: +31 (0)20 3 30 60 30
www.thetimeshotel.nl

Tram 1, 2, 5 Dam
13, 14, 17 Westermarkt

Prices: $$$

MAP N° 6

Hinter der Fassade des denkmalgeschützten Flaschengiebelhauses wird der Gast von einer modernen, aber gleichzeitig gemütlichen Atmosphäre überrascht. Das kleine, persönliche Hotel überzeugt mit zeitgemäßer Einrichtung und einer erstklassigen Lage an der Herengracht. Die Zimmer sind geprägt von ruhigen, warmen Farbtönen und alten holländischen Meistern an der Wand im XXL-Format. Shops, Restaurants und Kneipen sind zu Fuß bequem erreichbar.

INTERCONTINENTAL AMSTEL AMSTERDAM

Professor Tulpplein 1 // Oost
Tel.: +31 (0)20 6 22 60 60
www.amsterdam.intercontinental.com

Metro 51, 53, 54 Weesperplein
Tram 7, 10 Weesperplein

Prices: $$$$

MAP N°

Countless celebrities have stayed at the InterContinental Amstel Amsterdam. This "grand old lady" on the Amstel River has boasted the best address in the city since 1867. The elegant rooms and suites feature either a classical French or Dutch style interior. The hotel naturally includes a fitness club, sauna, and indoor pool. La Rive restaurant, awarded one Michelin star, is excellent. The terrace along the Amstel River is considered to be the most beautiful in Amsterdam.

Unzählige Prominente haben bereits im InterContinental Amstel Amsterdam logiert. Seit 1867 ist die „Grand Old Lady" an der Amstel die beste Adresse der Stadt. Die Zimmer und Suiten sind elegant im klassisch-französischen oder holländischen Stil gestaltet. Fitnessbereich, Sauna und ein überdachter Pool fehlen nicht. Exzellent ist auch das Restaurant La Rive, ausgezeichnet mit einem Michelinstern. Und die Terrasse am Amstelufer gilt als die schönste Amsterdams.

HOTELS

DE FILOSOOF

Anna van den Vondelstraat 6
Oud-Zuid
Tel.: +31 (0)20 6 83 30 13
www.sandton.eu/amsterdam

Tram 1 Jan Peter Heijestraat

Prices: $$$

Wittgenstein, Freud, Da Vinci, Epicurus—each of the 38 rooms and suites is dedicated to a different thinker or philosophical topic. Every room is different, yet they all feature vibrant colors: blue, red, and purple, from carpet to wallpaper. The style is equally as bold, ranging from baroque to classic to modern. Perhaps designers were inspired by the environment because the hotel is located close to the Museumkwartier district, Amsterdam's center for art and culture.

Wittgenstein, Freud, Da Vinci, Epikur – jedes der 38 Zimmer und Suiten ist einem anderen Denker oder philosophischen Thema gewidmet. Kein Zimmer gleicht dem anderen. Jedes ist in kräftigen Farben gehalten: Blau, Rot, Lila – vom Teppich bis zur Tapete. Genauso bunt ist auch der Stil: von Barock über klassisch bis hin zu modern. Inspiriert wurden die Designer vielleicht auch von der Umgebung, denn das Hotel liegt nahe dem Museumkwartier, Amsterdams Zentrum für Kunst und Kultur.

MUSEUM SUITES

Willemsparkweg 113 // Oud-Zuid
Tel.: +31 (0)20 3 31 83 00
www.museumsuites.com

Tram 2 Jacob Obrechtstraat

Prices: $$$

This elegant boutique hotel has only four suites, all very roomy with their own character inspired by great Dutch painters. The Rembrandt Suite features a classic interior with the light and dark color contrasts so typical for the work of this master. The Mondriaan Suite has a contemporary design with clear lines and vibrant colors. Romantics prefer the Vermeer or the Van Gogh Suite, both of which are bright, rustic, and sunny.

Das elegante Boutiquehotel hat lediglich vier Suiten, alle sehr geräumig und mit eigenem Charakter, inspiriert von den großen holländischen Malern. Die Rembrandt-Suite hat ein klassisches Interieur mit hellen und dunklen Farbkontrasten, die typisch für Gemälde des Meisters sind. Modernes Design bietet die Mondriaan-Suite, geprägt von klaren Linien und kräftigen Farben. Romantiker bevorzugen die Vermeer- oder die Van-Gogh-Suite: hell, ländlich und sonnig.

PARK HOTEL

Stadhouderskade 25 // Oud-Zuid
Tel.: +31 (0)20 6 71 12 22
www.parkhotel.nl

Tram 2, 5 Hobbemastraat
1 Stadhouderskade

Prices: $$$

MAP N°

As one of the most popular design hotels in the city, the four-star Park Hotel has reinvented the lobby: In the spacious "living room," comfortable designer chairs and lounge sofas arranged in front of a fireplace provide an inviting spot to relax. The modern yet warm style and luxurious furnishings can also be found in the rooms and suites. Guests can look forward to sleeping on high-quality mattresses, and the center of the city is just a stone's throw away.

Definitiv eines der beliebtesten Designhotels der Stadt. Das Vier-Sterne-Haus
hat dem Begriff Lobby neues Leben eingehaucht: Im großzügigen „Living Room"
laden komfortable Designstühle und Loungesofas rund um einen Kamin zum
Verweilen ein. Der moderne, aber warme Stil und die luxuriöse Ausstattung
setzen sich in den Zimmern und Suiten fort. Man schläft auf hochwertigen
Matratzen. Und das Zentrum der Stadt ist nur einen Steinwurf entfernt.

THE COLLEGE HOTEL

Roelof Hartstraat 1 // Oud-Zuid
Tel.: +31 (0)20 5 71 15 11
www.thecollegehotel.com

Tram 3, 5, 12, 24 Roelof Hartplein

Prices: $$$$

MAP N°

A special initiative and a unique concept: Students from hotel management schools are trained at The College Hotel. This likeable establishment has 40 rooms and is located in a brick structure that was built as a school in 1895. The interior design has a modern-classic slant with all the comforts you might expect from a four-star hotel. The former gymnasium now serves as a restaurant, while the former school yard was transformed into an inviting terrace.

Eine besondere Initiative und einmaliges Konzept: Im College Hotel
werden Studenten der Hotelfachschulen ausgebildet. Das sympathische
Haus hat 40 Zimmer und befindet sich in einem Backsteingebäude, das
1895 als Schule erbaut wurde. Die Einrichtung ist modern-klassisch, mit
allem Komfort, den man von einem Vier-Sterne-Hotel erwarten kann.
Die alte Sporthalle dient heute als Restaurant, der ehemalige Schulhof
wurde in eine einladende Terrasse umgewandelt.

Earlier guests of the Lloyd didn't spend the night voluntarily: It was used as a prison for many decades. However, this striking building in the Eastern Docklands was originally constructed in 1921 as a luxury hotel for émigrés. The spirit of the past hasn't disappeared altogether: An overnight stay at the Lloyd Hotel is a special experience. Organized into categories from one to five stars, rooms here are all different and furnished by Dutch designers in a retro style.

LLOYD HOTEL

Oostelijke Handelskade 34 // Zeeburg
Tel.: +31 (0)20 5 61 36 36
www.lloydhotel.com

Tram 10, 26 Rietlandpark

Prices: $$$

MAP N° 12

Wer früher im Lloyd logierte, tat das nicht freiwillig: Es diente jahrzehnte-
lang als Gefängnis. Ursprünglich jedoch wurde das markante Gebäude
im östlichen Hafengebiet 1921 als Luxushotel für Auswanderer erbaut.
Der Geist der Vergangenheit ist nicht ganz verschwunden: Eine
Übernachtung im Lloyd ist ein besonderes Erlebnis. Jedes Zimmer ist
anders, unterteilt in ein bis fünf Sterne und von niederländischen
Designern im Retrostil eingerichtet.

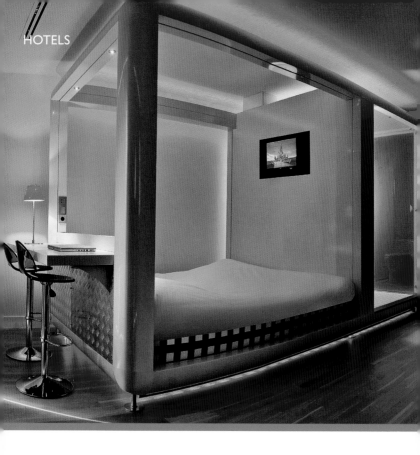

Spend the night in a cube, and, depending on your mood, illuminate the room in "Mellow Yellow," "Romantic Red," or "Cool Blue." Qbic is one of the city's latest design hotels, and its innovative furnishings have clearly been inspired by four-poster beds. The cube is bedroom, bathroom, and sitting area all in one. All rooms include Wi-Fi, air conditioning, LCD TV, and a safe. The modern address close to Amsterdam's World Trade Center fits right in with this creative hotel.

QBIC HOTEL AMSTERDAM

Mathijs Vermeulenpad 1 // Zuid
Tel.: +31 (900) 7 46 83 57
www.qbichotels.com

Tram 5 Zuid
Metro 50, 51 Zuid

Prices: $$

MAP N° **13**

Übernachten in einem Kubus und je nach Lust und Laune wird das Zimmer in „Mellow Yellow", „Romantic Red" oder „Cool Blue" beleuchtet. Qbic ist eines der jüngsten Designhotels der Stadt und hat sich bei der innovativen Einrichtung offensichtlich vom guten alten Himmelbett inspirieren lassen. Der Kubus ist Schlafraum, Badezimmer und Sitzecke zugleich. Wi-Fi, Klima-anlage, LCD-TV und ein Safe gehören zum Standard. Zum kreativen Hotel passt die moderne Adresse nahe dem Amsterdam World Trade Center.

Zuiver—Dutch for "pure"—offers relaxation for the body, mind, and spirit. The hotel is part of a 140,000 sq. ft. wellness complex. Though somewhat austere from the outside, on the inside the spa surprises with its luxurious and straightforward design. After visiting the sauna, steam bath, and swimming pool, you can relax in one of the 31 contemporary rooms. Zuiver is located on the edge of the Amsterdamse Bos recreation area, away from the city center, and as a result is quiet and affordable.

ZUIVER

Koenenkade 8 // Zuid
Tel.: +31 (0)20 3 01 07 10
www.zuiveramsterdam.nl

Bus 170, 172 Koenenkade

Prices: $$

MAP N° **14**

Zuiver – niederländisch für pur – bietet Entspannung für Körper,
Geist und Seele. Das Hotel ist Teil eines 13 000 m² großen Wellness-
Komplexes. Etwas nüchtern von außen, aber innen überrascht das Spa
mit seinem luxuriösen und klaren Design. Nach einem Besuch der
Sauna, des Dampfbads und der Swimmingpools kann man in einem
der 31 modern gestalteten Zimmer ausspannen. Zuiver liegt am
Rand des Erholungsgebiets Amsterdamse Bos, abseits vom Zentrum,
dafür ist es aber ruhig und preisgünstig.

RESTAURANTS +CAFÉS

COOL
AMSTERDAM

Restaurant

The city government has new plans for the historic downtown area, which has given new impetus to the red light district. Restaurant ANNA, which has made a name for itself in a very short period of time, fits right in with this concept. From the tables to the open kitchen, everything has a simple, modern style that matches the restaurant's motto of offering excellent cuisine at a moderate price in a relaxed atmosphere. In the summer, guests can dine on the terrace in the square.

ANNA

Warmoesstraat 111 // Centrum
Tel.: +31 (0)20 4 28 11 11
www.restaurantanna.nl

Mon–Fri noon to 3 pm
and 6 pm to 10.30 pm
Sat 6 pm to 10.30 pm

Tram 4, 9, 16, 24, 25 Dam

Prices: $$$
Cuisine: European

MAP N° 15

Mit der historischen Innenstadt hat die Stadtverwaltung neue Pläne, wodurch das Rotlichtviertel neue Impulse bekam und bekommt. In dieses Konzept passt das Restaurant ANNA, das sich in kurzer Zeit einen Namen gemacht hat. Von den Tischen bis hin zur offenen Küche zeichnet sich alles durch einen einfachen, modernen Stil aus, der zum Motto des Hauses passt: erstklassiges Essen zu moderaten Preisen in einer ungezwungenen Atmosphäre. Im Sommer kann man auf der Terrasse am Platz speisen.

BRIDGES

Oudezijds Voorburgwal 197
Centrum
Tel.: +31 (0)20 5 55 35 60
www.bridgesrestaurant.nl

Breakfast: daily 6.30 am to 10.30 am,
Sat, Sun 6.30 am to 11 am
Lunch: daily noon to 3 pm,
Sat, Sun from 12.30 pm
Dinner: daily 6 pm to 11 pm

Tram 4, 9, 14, 16, 24, 25 Spui

Prices: $$$$
Cuisine: French, Fish, International

MAP N° **16**

When guests enter Bridges, they are greeted with a vibrant mural by
Karel Appel. In fact, the restaurant's entire interior decor was inspired
by the expressionistic style of this famous Amsterdam artist, a member
of the Cobra artist's group. Located in the exclusive The Grand hotel,
the restaurant has become noted for its fresh fish prepared in classic
French style. According to gourmet critics and Internet forums, it is one
of the best restaurants in Amsterdam.

Begrüßt wird der Gast im Bridges von einem bunten Wandgemälde von Karel Appel. Die gesamte Einrichtung des Restaurants wurde vom expressionistischen Stil dieses bekannten Amsterdamer Malers aus der Künstlergruppe Cobra inspiriert. Gerühmt wird das Lokal, gelegen im exklusiven Hotel The Grand, wegen des frischen Fischs, der auf klassische französische Art zubereitet wird. Laut Gourmetkritikern und Internetforen eines der besten Restaurants der Stadt.

D'VIJFF VLIEGHEN

49

Spuistraat 294–302 // Centrum
Tel.: +31 (0)20 5 30 40 60
www.dininginamsterdam.nl

Daily 6 pm to 10 pm

Tram 1, 2, 5 Spui

Prices: $$$
Cuisine: Dutch

This long-established restaurant is an institution in Amsterdam. Here, you will find yourself dining between famous blue Delft tiles, rustic wooden furniture, and old paintings. If you order a surprise menu, the chef will decide what sort of hearty Dutch cuisine to offer you. The restaurant has hosted many prominent guests who have been immortalized on the chairs. You never know—you may find yourself occupying the same seat as Mick Jagger or Bruce Springsteen.

Dieses alteingesessene Restaurant ist eine Institution in der Stadt. Hier speist man zwischen den berühmten blauen Fliesen aus Delft, rustikalen Holzmöbeln und alten Gemälden. Wer ein Überraschungsmenü bestellt, der überlässt dem Koch die Auswahl aus der deftigen holländischen Küche. Das Restaurant hat so manchen prominenten Gast empfangen, der auf dem Stuhl verewigt wurde. So sitzt man vielleicht zufällig auf demselben Platz wie Mick Jagger oder Bruce Springsteen.

17

RESTAURANTS
+CAFÉS

LUCIUS

Spuistraat 247 // Centrum
Tel.: +31 (0)20 6 24 18 31
www.lucius.nl

Daily 5 pm to midnight

Tram 1, 2, 5 Spui

Prices: $$$
Cuisine: Fish

Lucius is the opposite of a stylized designer restaurant. The conventional Dutch/French bistro-style atmosphere is enjoying a hip rebirth thanks to the popular retro trend. The kitchen features fresh, traditional cuisine with tried-and-true dishes such as fish soup and a mixed fish platter. The chef has even added Dutch herring with raw onions to the menu. The fish is served with Dutch corn schnapps—just the thing for cool guys.

Das Lucius ist das Gegenteil eines gestylten Designrestaurants. Das Ambiente ist konventionell im holländisch-französischen Bistrostil, der im Retrotrend aber gerade wieder angesagt ist. Die Küche setzt auf Tradition und Frische mit altbewährten Gerichten wie Fischsuppe oder gemischter Fischplatte. Der Chef hat es sogar gewagt, den holländischen Hering mit rohen Zwiebeln auf die Menükarte zu setzen. Serviert wird der Fisch mit holländischem Korn – etwas für coole Typen.

STANISLAVSKI

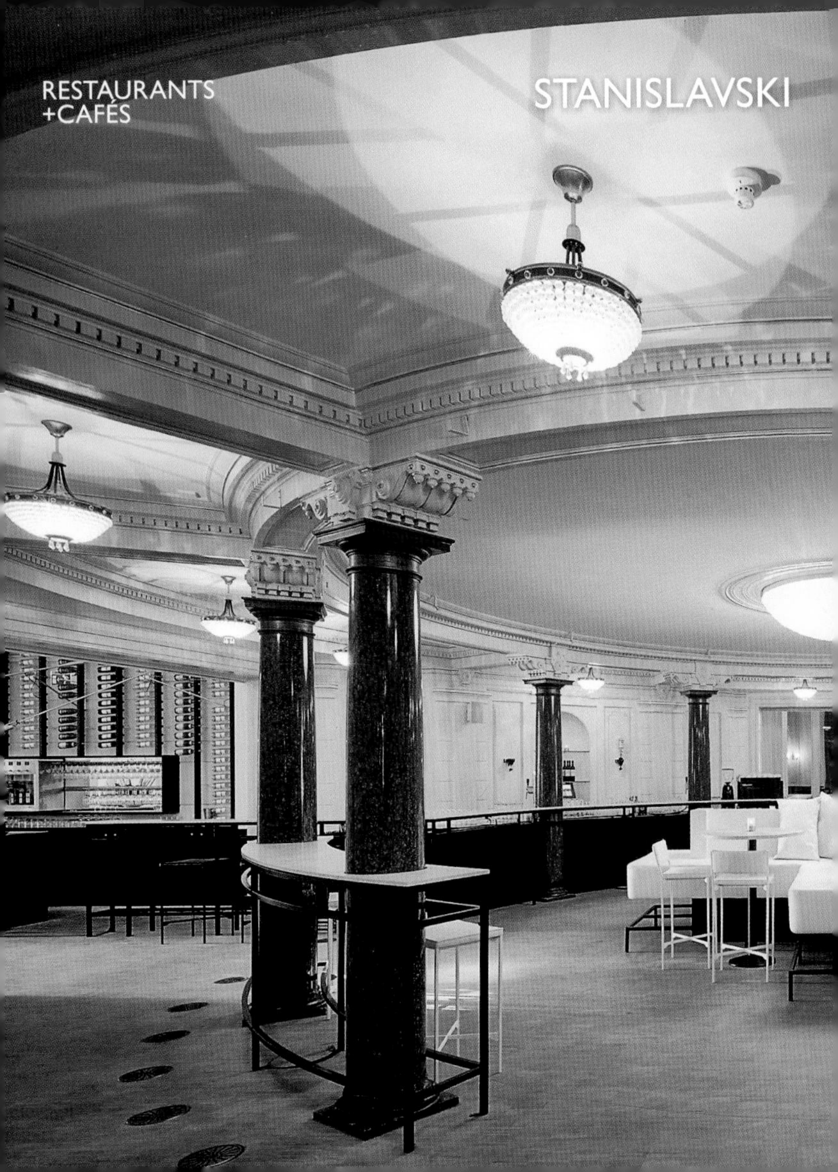

Leidseplein 26 // Centrum
Tel.: +31 (0)20 7 95 99 95
www.stanislavski.nl

Mon–Sat 9 am to 11 pm
Sun 10 am to 11 pm

Tram 1, 2, 5, 7, 10 Leidseplein

Prices: $$
Cuisine: International

Art, culture, and good cuisine. In the foyer of the Stadsschouwburg
municipal theater, the Stanislavski is the perfect place to relax. Its style
is modern, and the atmosphere casual and cosmopolitan. Stairs lead to
the Ajax foyer, known throughout Holland, and up to the Ajax terrace
with its gorgeous view of the lively Leidseplein. The terrace is where
Ajax soccer players have been cheered, prominent artists celebrated,
and international guests received.

Kunst, Kultur und gute Küche. Das Stanislavski im Foyer der Stads-
schouwburg (Stadttheater) ist genau das richtige Lokal, um zu entspannen.
Der Stil ist modern, das Ambiente lässig und kosmopolitisch. Eine Treppe
führt zum landesweit bekannten Ajaxfoyer und zur Ajaxterrasse
hinauf, von wo aus man einen schönen Blick auf den lebendigen Leidseplein
hat. Hier oben wurden die Ajax-Fußballspieler bejubelt, renommierte
Künstler gefeiert und internationale Gäste empfangen.

ZOUTHAVEN

Piet Heinkade 1 // Centrum
Tel.: +31 (0)20 7 88 20 90
www.zouthaven.nl

Daily 10.30 am to 11 pm

Tram 26 Muziekgebouw

Prices: $$$
Cuisine: Fish

MAP N° **20**

The views of the water and the boats are arresting. The cool white interior feels rather austere but matches the structure. The restaurant is located in the modern Muziekgebouw aan 't IJ building in Amsterdam's Eastern Docklands and focuses on fish dishes. Diners can savor raw oysters and other seafood at the trendy Raw Bar. For the sake of the environment, the restaurant serves some fish products that carry the blue MSC seal, which means that you can eat here without feeling guilty.

Die Aussicht auf das Wasser und die Schiffe überzeugt sofort. Das Interieur im coolen Weiß wirkt etwas clean, passt aber zum Gebäude. Das Restaurant befindet sich im modernen Muziekgebouw aan 't IJ im östlichen Hafenviertel. Der Fokus liegt auf Fischgerichten. An der trendy Raw Bar genießt man rohe Austern und andere Meeresfrüchte. Der Umwelt zuliebe werden teilweise Fischprodukte serviert, die das blaue MSC-Siegel tragen. Man kann hier also mit gutem Gewissen essen.

RESTAURANTS
+CAFÉS

STORK

This supersized café restaurant is a bit off the beaten track in an industrial area in the Noord district. Fans still make their way to Stork, whether it's to enjoy the fresh fish or the industrial architecture. The conversion of a factory building into a restaurant reflects current developments in the city. When the weather is nice, diners can sit right on the water. It is the perfect spot to take in the view of Amsterdam, sip a drink, and listen to jazz or lounge music playing in the background—simply relaxing.

STORK

Gedempt Hamerkanaal 96 // Noord
Tel.: +31 (0)20 6 34 40 00
www.restaurantstork.nl

Daily from 11 am

Ferry boat 902 IJplein
Bus 38, 105, 109, 361, 363, 611, 624
Havikslaan

Prices: $$$
Cuisine: International

MAP N° 21

Dieses Café-Restaurant in XXL-Format liegt etwas abseits auf einem Industriegelände im Stadtteil Noord. Liebhaber finden trotzdem den Weg ins Stork, sei es wegen des frischen Fischs, sei es wegen der Industriearchitektur. Die Umwidmung einer Fabrikhalle in ein Restaurant passt zu den aktuellen Entwicklungen in der Stadt. Bei gutem Wetter kann man direkt am Wasser sitzen. Man blickt dabei auf Amsterdam, nippt am Drink und lauscht im Hintergrund der Jazz- oder Loungemusik – einfach entspannend.

Amsterdam's old municipal nursery was saved from demolition at the last minute by a Michelin-starred chef with a vision. De Kas—Dutch for greenhouse—is a unique restaurant that features organic herbs and vegetables from its own garden. Seasonal dishes—either vegetarian or combined with meat or fish—draw upon ingredients harvested from the restaurant's garden and are always of the highest quality. Guests enjoy the pleasant ambience and an idyllic location in a city park.

DE KAS

Kamerlingh Onneslaan 3 // Oost
Tel.: +31 (0)20 4 62 45 63
www.restaurantdekas.nl

Lunch: Mon–Fri noon to 2 pm
Dinner: Mon–Sat 6.30 pm to 10 pm

Tram 9, Bus 41, Bus 357 Hogeweg

Prices: $$$
Cuisine: Mediterranean

MAP N° **22**

In letzter Minute wurde die alte Stadtgärtnerei vor dem Abbruch
bewahrt, gerettet von einem Sternekoch mit Vision. De Kas – nieder-
ländisch für Gewächshaus – ist ein einzigartiges Restaurant mit bio-
logischem Eigenanbau von Gemüse und Kräutern. Was auf den Tisch
kommt, sind wechselnde Gerichte aus eigener Ernte, vegetarisch oder
kombiniert mit Fleisch oder Fisch, aber immer auf Spitzenniveau. Dazu
das angenehme Ambiente und die idyllische Lage in einem Stadtpark.

DE YSBREEKER

Weesperzijde 23 // Oost
Tel.: +31 (0)20 4 68 18 08
www.deysbreeker.nl

Mon–Thu 8 am to 1 am
Fri–Sat 8 am to 2 am

Tram 3 Wibautstraat

Prices: $$
Cuisine: Café

MAP N° **23**

It seems as if you can often find half of Amsterdam along this quiet stretch of the Amstel River. The atmosphere is relaxed, and the crowd is mixed. De Ysbreeker is located in a monumental building and is particularly popular because of its street terrace. When the sun shines, the chairs and tables along the sidewalk or overlooking the water fill quickly. Here you can start the day over breakfast and wind up the evening in good company over a glass of wine or regional beer.

Es scheint so, als wäre halb Amsterdam regelmäßig an diesem ruhigen Teil der Amstel zu finden. Die Atmosphäre ist lässig, das Publikum gemischt. De Ysbreeker befindet sich in einem monumentalen Gebäude und ist vor allem wegen seiner Straßenterrasse beliebt. Die Stühle und Tische auf dem Gehsteig oder am Wasser sind bei den ersten Sonnenstrahlen schnell belegt. Hier beginnt man mit dem Frühstück und endet am Abend in guter Gesellschaft bei einem Glas Wein oder regionalem Bier.

Westerdoksplein 20 // Centrum
Tel.: +31 (0)20 6 20 10 10
www.open.nl

Mon–Fri noon to 1 am, Sat 5 pm to 1 am

Bus 48 Westerdoksdijk

Prices: $$
Cuisine: European

Open's architecture is fascinating, and the restaurant blends history with an urban attitude toward life: A railroad bridge dating from 1920 forms a solid foundation and the modern structure consists of glass. The cuisine is contemporary and offers an affordable two-course menu for lunch. The white interior features vibrant dashes of color, and guests can relax on apple-green sofas and take in the magnificent water view—a panorama that is truly magical.

Das Open besticht durch seine ausgefallene Architektur und präsentiert sich in einer Mischung aus Geschichte und urbanem Lebensgefühl: Eine Eisenbahnbrücke von 1920 formt die solide Basis, der moderne Aufbau besteht aus Glas. Die Küche ist zeitgemäß und bietet zur Mittagszeit ein preisgünstiges Zwei-Gänge-Menü. Im weißen Interieur mit bunten Farbtupfern genießt der Gast auf apfelgrünen Sofas die herrliche Aussicht auf das Wasser – ein Panorama zum Träumen.

POMPSTATION

Zeeburgerdijk 52 // Zeeburg
Tel.: +31 (0)20 6 92 28 88
www.pompstation.nu

Tue–Sat from 5 pm
in summer from 3 pm

Tram 14 Zeeburgerdijk

Prices: $$
Cuisine: Steaks

MAP N° **25**

Featuring the brick style of the Amsterdam school of architecture, a water pumping station from 1912 houses this unique restaurant in a multicultural area. Steel, glass, wood, and tiles were used in the interior to retain the building's character. The result is an amazing industrial look which has gone over well with a wide audience. Pompstation specializes in American-style broiled steaks. Live performances take place regularly and create a fantastic atmosphere.

Ein Pumpenhaus von 1912 im Backstein-Stil der Amsterdamer Schule bietet Unterkunft für dieses Restaurant in einem multikulturellen Viertel. Um den Charakter zu erhalten, wurden für die Inneneinrichtung Stahl, Glas, Holz und Fliesen verwendet. Das Resultat ist ein wunderbarer industrieller Look, der bei einem breiten Publikum ankommt. Pompstation hat sich auf Steaks vom amerikanischen Grill (Broiler) spezialisiert. Live-auftritte sorgen regelmäßig für großartige Stimmung.

Scheldeplein 4 // Zuid
Tel.: +31 (0)20 6 75 15 83
www.visaandeschelde.nl

Lunch: Mon–Fri noon to 2.30 pm
Dinner: daily 5.30 pm to 11 pm

Tram 4 Dintelstraat
12, 25 Scheldestraat
Bus 65, 612 Scheldeplein

Prices: $$$$
Cuisine: Fish, Dutch, French

This specialty restaurant is located in the chic city district of Zuid close to the exhibition grounds. At Visaandeschelde, the interior design is a contemporary blend of old and new. Traditional white tiles on the walls are interspersed with tiles decorated with fishing motifs in Delft blue. A menu featuring fish and seafood as well as meat is offered for lunch and dinner. The open kitchen allows guests to see the passion that goes into the preparation of the dishes.

In der Nähe des Messegeländes, im schicken Stadtteil Zuid gelegenes Spezialitätenrestaurant. Bei der Einrichtung wurden Altes und Neues zeitgemäß kombiniert. Für die Wände wurden traditionelle weiße Fliesen verwendet, von Motiven aus der Fischerei im delftblauen Design unterbrochen. Zur Mittagszeit und am Abend wird jeweils ein Menü mit Fisch und Meeresfrüchten angeboten. Aber in der einsehbaren Küche wird mit viel Leidenschaft auch Fleisch zubereitet.

SHOPS

BLOEMENMARKT

Singel // Centrum
Tel.: +31 (0)20 6 25 82 82

Daily 9 am to 5.30 pm
Sun from 11 am

Tram 4, 9, 16, 24, 25 Muntplein

Prices: $

MAP N° 27

Thanks to the popular hit song, almost everyone is familiar with tulips from Amsterdam. The flower market on the Singel draws hoards of visitors looking for these colorful spring flowers. If it's the wrong season to find tulips in bloom, the market sells tulip bulbs, and they sell like hotcakes. Simply stated, the ocean of flower bouquets arrayed in front of stalls is simply enchanting, and the colors and fragrances will gladden your heart and lift your mood.

Tulpen aus Amsterdam kennt fast jeder, zumindest aus dem weltberühmten Schlager. Auf der Suche nach den bunten Frühlingsblumen zieht es Scharen von Besuchern zum Blumenmarkt an der Singel. Gibt es saisonbedingt keine blühenden Tulpen, werden eben die Tulpenzwiebeln verkauft, und die gehen weg wie warme Semmeln. Mal ganz ehrlich: Das Meer an Blumensträußen vor den Ständen ist einfach bezaubernd und die Farben und Düfte erfreuen das Herz und heben die Laune.

DE KAASKAMER

Runstraat 7 // Centrum
Tel.: +31 (0)20 6 23 34 83
www.kaaskamer.nl

Mon noon to 6 pm,
Tue–Fri 9 am to 6 pm
Sat 9 am to 5 pm
Sun noon to 5 pm

Tram 1, 2, 5 Spui

Prices: $

MAP N° 28

Cheese lovers don't have it easy downtown because typical cheese stores are hard to find. In the "9 Straatjes" (9 Streets) district, you'll hit the jackpot: De Kaaskamer features over 400 different types of cheese stacked floor to ceiling—Dutch farmhouse cheese; cheese with caraway seeds, nettles, or garlic; goat cheese and sheep's cheese. Perhaps a young, creamy cheese? Or do you prefer a full-flavored hard cheese? As is the custom in Holland, you can sample cheese for free.

Käseliebhaber haben es im Zentrum nicht leicht, denn typische Käseläden sind schwer zu finden. Fündig wird man im Viertel „9 Straatjes" (Neun Gassen): In der Kaaskamer stapeln sich über 400 unterschiedliche Käsesorten vom Boden bis zur Decke. Holländischer Bauernkäse, Käse mit Kümmel, Brennesseln oder Knoblauch, Ziegen- und Schafskäse. Darf es ein junger, cremiger Käse sein? Oder lieber ein harter, würziger? Einfach gratis kosten, denn das ist Brauch in Holland.

FLORIS VAN BOMMEL

Singel 439–441 // Centrum
Tel.: +31 (0)20 6 25 42 77
www.florisvanbommel.nl

Mon, Sun 1 pm to 6 pm
Tue–Sat 10 am to 6 pm, Thu to 9 pm

Tram 1,2, 5 Koningsplein

Prices: $$$

For decades, the Van Bommel brand has stood for classic men's business shoes. In recent years, the latest generation of this family-owned operation has put its own stamp on the brand. After finding success in Berlin and Antwerp, they have finally opened a branch in their native country in a prime location on the Singel. The collection combines sports and classics, sneakers and brogues, but all feature bold colors or vibrant color contrasts.

Die Marke Van Bommel steht seit Jahrzehnten für klassische Business-schuhe für den Herrn. Nun hat die jüngste Generation des Familien-betriebs einen neuen Stil auf den Markt gebracht. Erst nach dem Erfolg in Berlin und Antwerpen wurde eine Filiale im Heimatland eröffnet, in bester Lage an der Singel. Die Kollektion kombiniert Sport und Klassik, Sneakers mit Brogues, aber immer in frechen Farben oder mit kräftigen Farbkontrasten.

Warmoesstraat 67 // Centrum
Tel.: +31 (0)20 6 24 06 83
www.geels.nl

Mon–Sat 9 am to 6 pm

Tram 4, 9, 16, 24, 25 Dam

Prices: $

The enticing smell of freshly roasted coffee beans and fragrant teas
greet the customers at Geels & Co. Known far beyond Amsterdam,
this old family company in the heart of the city has specialized in coffee
and tea since 1864. Over the years, little has changed in the museum-like
furnishings. As in grandma's day, tea is still weighed and packaged for
customers, coffee is freshly ground and hermetically sealed, and patrons
can always rely on expert advice.

Herrliche Aromen von frisch gerösteten Kaffeebohnen und blumigen
Teesorten empfangen die Kunden von Geels & Co. Das alte Familien-
unternehmen im Herzen von Amsterdam ist seit 1864 auf Kaffee und
Tee spezialisiert und bis weit über die Stadtgrenzen hinaus bekannt.
An der musealen Einrichtung hat sich wenig geändert. Wie zu Omas
Zeiten wird der Tee für den Kunden abgewogen und verpackt, der
Kaffee frisch gemahlen und luftdicht verschlossen. Und dazu gibt es
fachkundige Beratung.

His shoes are award winning, and an exhibition has been dedicated to his designs, his entire collection, and his career. Jan Jansen launched his career in Rome, where he worked for famous fashion houses such as Dior. Over the years, Jansen has opened several shoe stores in Holland. His stores draw inspiration for their furnishings from living rooms. The store on Rokin is designed to look like an attic, and idiosyncratic, timeless models are presented under the wooden beams.

JAN JANSEN

Rokin 42 // Centrum
Tel.: +31 (0)20 6 25 13 50
www.janjansen.nl

Tue–Sat 10 am to 6 pm

Tram 4, 9, 14, 16, 24, 25 Dam

Prices: $$$$

MAP N° **31**

Seine Schuhe sind preisgekrönt, dem Design, seiner Gesamtkollektion und seiner Karriere wurde sogar eine Ausstellung gewidmet. Jan Jansen begann seine Laufbahn in Rom, arbeitete für bekannte Modehäuser wie Dior und hat im Lauf der Jahre mehrere Schuhgeschäfte in Holland eröffnet. Wohnräume sind die Inspiration für die Einrichtung der Geschäfte. Der Laden am Rokin wurde einem Dachboden nachempfunden. Unter den Holzbalken werden eigensinnige, zeitlose Modelle präsentiert.

SHOPS

LAURA DOLS

Wolvenstraat 7 // Centrum
Tel.: +31 (0)20 6 24 90 66
www.lauradols.nl

Daily 11 am to 6 pm, Thu to 9 pm
Sun noon to 6 pm

Tram 1, 2, 5 Spui

Prices: $$

Are you looking for a stunning cocktail dress or a red-carpet-worthy evening gown for a special evening? At Laura Dols you'll find the glamorous piece of clothing you're looking for, along with the right handbag and accessories to go with it. This vintage store features exclusive second-hand fashion from the 1950s. With princess-style dresses, Laura Dols is heaven on earth even for their youngest customers. Be patient and come prepared to spend some time browsing.

Auf der Suche nach einem umwerfenden Cocktailkleid oder einer Galarobe im Hollywoodstil für einen speziellen Abend? Bei Laura Dols entdecken Sie das glamouröse Stück und die richtige Tasche und Accessoires gleich dazu. Exklusive Secondhandmode aus den 50er Jahren steht im Vintage-Laden im Vordergrund. Auch für die Kleinsten ist Laura Dols der Himmel auf Erde, mit Kleidern im Prinzessinnenlook. Ein wenig Zeit und Geduld zum Stöbern sollte man mitbringen.

Amsterdam's landmark city center does not offer any room for a modern shopping mall. Magna Plaza is the exception, and it did not come into being until the century-old main post office became vacant. This monumental brick building is very striking. In the central hall and distributed over three floors, you will encounter various fashion stores featuring international labels, sportswear, shoes, jewelry, and other accessories.

MAGNA PLAZA

Nieuwezijds Voorburgwal 182
Centrum
Tel.: +31 (0)20 4 21 17 17
www.magnaplaza.nl

Mon 11 am to 7 pm
Tue–Sat 10 am to 7 pm,
Thu to 9 pm
Sun noon to 7 pm

Tram 1, 2, 5, 13, 14, 17 Dam

Prices: $$$

MAP N° 33

Das denkmalgeschützte Stadtzentrum bietet keinen Platz für eine moderne Shoppingmall. Magna Plaza ist die Ausnahme und erst entstanden, als das über 100 Jahre alte Hauptpostamt frei wurde. Das monumentale Backsteingebäude fällt gleich ins Auge. In der zentralen Halle und verteilt auf drei Etagen findet man mehrere Modegeschäfte mit internationalen Labels, Sportbekleidung, Schuhen, Schmuck und anderen Accessoires.

MENDO

Berenstraat 11 // Centrum
Tel.: +31 (0)20 6 12 12 16
www.mendo.nl

Mon–Sat noon to 5.30 pm
Sun 1 pm to 5 pm

Tram 1, 2, 5 Spui
13, 14, 17 Westermarkt

Prices: $$$

MAP N° 34

MENDO bookstore will send art book enthusiasts into raptures. Architecture, design, photography, fashion, music—MENDO has a huge selection of high-quality creative books from around the world. Thanks also to the store's stylish interior design featuring dark colors and shiny ball lamps, MENDO is considered to be one of the top bookstores in Amsterdam. The location is spot on as well: in the trendy "Negen Straatjes" shopping district in the city center.

Der Buchladen MENDO versetzt Liebhaber von Kunstbüchern in
Verzückung. Architektur, Design, Fotografie, Fashion, Musik – das
Angebot an internationalen, hochwertigen und kreativen Büchern ist
enorm. Aber ebenso wegen der stylischen Inneneinrichtung mit
dunklen Farben und glänzenden Kugellampen gilt MENDO als einer
der Topbuchläden der Stadt. Auch die Lage passt: im trendigen
Einkaufsviertel „Negen Straatjes" im Zentrum.

NUKUHIVA

Haarlemmerstraat 36 // Centrum
Tel.: +31 (0)20 4 20 94 83
www.nukuhiva.nl

Mon, Sun noon to 6 pm
Tue–Sat 10 am to 6 pm, Thu to 7 pm

Tram 1, 2, 4, 5, 9, 16, 17, 24, 25, 26
Centraal Station

Prices: $$$

MAP N° 35

Nukuhiva demonstrates just how cool and beautiful eco-fashion can
be. With its clear design sense, this boutique is an initiative of Dutch
TV host and travel journalist Floortje Dessing. The fashion labels
carried by the store are innovative and selected based on their
sustainability or social commitment. The range of products emphasizes
fashions made from eco-friendly and recycled materials, from elegant
blouses to rugged jeans to exotic jewelry.

Wie cool und schön Öko-Mode aussehen kann, zeigt Nukuhiva. Die Boutique mit ihrem klaren Design ist eine Initiative der niederländischen Fernsehmoderatorin und Reisejournalistin Floortje Dessing. Die geführten Modelabels sind innovativ und werden aufgrund von Nachhaltigkeit oder sozialem Engagement ausgewählt. Mode aus Bio-Stoffen oder recycelten Materialien bestimmen das Sortiment, von der eleganten Bluse über robuste Jeans bis hin zu exotischem Schmuck.

Forget the usual souvenir stores! At Thinking of Holland located in the passenger terminal, souvenirs have taken on an entirely new meaning. At this modern store, you can purchase special souvenirs of Holland— gifts that are slightly different as well as creative. Items are made by contemporary Dutch designers, such as the award-winning umbrella by Senz or original t-shirts with animal imprints by Mingface.

THINKING OF HOLLAND

Piet Heinkade 23 // Centrum
Tel.: +31 (0)20 4 19 12 29
www.thinkingofholland.com

Daily 10 am to 7 pm

Tram 26 Passenger Terminal

Prices: $$

MAP N° 36

Vergessen Sie die üblichen Souvenirläden! Bei Thinking of Holland im Passagierterminal erhält der Begriff Souvenir eine ganz neue Bedeutung. In dem modernen Geschäft gibt es besondere Erinnerungen an Holland zu kaufen, das etwas andere, das kreative Geschenk. Die Produkte werden von zeitgenössischen niederländischen Designern gefertigt, wie der preisgekrönte Sturmregenschirm von Senz oder die originellen T-Shirts mit Tieraufdrucken von Mingface.

Delicate caramel with a hint of pepper, and sweet orange combined with cloves: Unlimited Delicious is famous throughout Amsterdam for its divine chocolates with exciting and daring flavor combinations. In this small shop on Haarlemmerstraat, everything revolves around chocolate. The cakes made with different kinds of chocolate are irresistible as well. And the truffles with surprising fillings are simply addictive. Hobby chocolatiers can take a workshop with the master.

UNLIMITED DELICIOUS

Haarlemmerstraat 122 // Centrum
Tel.: +31 (0)20 6 22 48 29
www.unlimiteddelicious.nl

Mon–Sat 9 am to 6 pm

Metro 51, 53, 54 Centraal Station
Tram 1, 2, 4, 5, 9, 13, 16,
17, 24, 25, 26 Centraal Station
3 Haarlemmerplein

Prices: $$

MAP N° 37

Zartes Karamell mit einem Hauch Pfeffer, süße Orange mit Nelken kombiniert – Unlimited Delicious ist für seine herrlichen Pralinen mit spannenden und gewagten Geschmacksrichtungen in der ganzen Stadt bekannt. Im kleinen Laden an der Haarlemmerstraat dreht sich alles um Schokolade. Unwiderstehlich sind auch die Torten mit Schokoladenvariationen. Und die Trüffel mit überraschenden Füllungen machen schlichtweg süchtig. Hobby-Chocolatiers können einen Workshop beim Meister belegen.

SHOPS

*Where does
Design begin?*

WENDYTROOST

YDU

Keizersgracht 447 // Centrum
Tel.: +31 (0)20 6 26 91 91
www.ydu.nl

Mon 1 pm to 6 pm
Tue–Sat 10 am to 6 pm
Thu 10 am to 8 pm

Tram 1, 2, 5 Keizersgracht

Prices: $$

The three letters in the store's name stand for Young Designers United.
This boutique on the Keizersgracht offers a platform for promising
Dutch fashion designers and gives these emerging talents the opportunity
to present their creations and reach customers. The boutique features
exclusive but wearable women's fashions and accessories of very high
quality and at affordable prices. The collection changes regularly, so it's
worth stopping by frequently.

Die drei Buchstaben stehen für Young Designers United. Die Boutique
an der Keizersgracht bietet vielversprechenden niederländischen
Modedesignern eine Plattform. Junge Talente bekommen so die Chance,
ihre Modelabels zu präsentieren und Kunden zu erreichen. Geboten
werden exklusive, aber tragbare Damenmode und Accessoires von
sehr guter Qualität und zu erschwinglichen Preisen. Die Kollektion
wechselt regelmäßig, da schaut man gerne öfter vorbei.

CLUBS, LOUNGES +BARS

COQL
AMSTERDAM

CLUBS,
LOUNGES
+BARS

AIR AMSTERDAM

Amstelstraat 24 // Centrum
Tel.: +31 (0)20 8 20 06 70
www.air.nl

Fri, Sat 11 pm to 5 am
Thu, Sun 23.30 pm to 4 am

Tram 4, 9, 14 Rembrandtplein

Prices: $$$

Close to the lively Rembrandtplein, AIR Amsterdam replaced the internationally renowned Club IT. Prominent Dutch designer Marcel Wanders is the force behind the stunning interior. The exclusive club stands for tolerance, diversity, creativity, and freedom, targets different audiences, and presents a variety of musical trends. The best way to find out what's happening in this cool location is to check its online program.

AIR Amsterdam nahe dem lebendigen Rembrandtplein ersetzte den über die Landesgrenzen hinaus bekannten Club IT. Die Einrichtung des renommierten holländischen Designers Marcel Wanders ist umwerfend. Der exklusive Club steht für viel Toleranz, Diversität, Kreativität und Freiheit, richtet sich an verschiedene Zielgruppen und präsentiert unterschiedliche Musikströmungen. Was in der coolen Location los ist, erfährt man am besten in seinem Online-Programm.

CLUBS,
LOUNGES
+BARS

BIMHUIS

BIMHUIS

Piet Heinkade 3 // Centrum
Tel.: +31 (0)20 7 88 21 88
www.bimhuis.nl

Daily (on concert nights)
6.30 pm to 1 am
Fri, Sat to 3 am

Tram 26 Muziekgebouw

Prices: $$

MAP N° **40**

Amsterdam's meeting place for the national and international jazz scene
has its origins in a furniture warehouse in 1974. Today, Bimhuis is
located in a black box that juts out spectacularly from the Muziek-
gebouw aan 't IJ. This club sets high standards for acoustics, interior
design, and atmosphere. The concert hall, the bar, and the restaurant
are all interconnected—which means that you can listen to jazz while
enjoying views of the water.

Amsterdams Treffpunkt für die nationale und internationale Jazzszene begann 1974 in einem Möbellager. Heute befindet sich das Bimhuis in der Black Box, die aus dem Muziekgebouw aan 't IJ spektakulär herausragt. Hier wurde ein Club geschaffen, der hohe Ansprüche sowohl an die Akustik als auch an das Raumdesign und die Atmosphäre stellt. Der Konzertsaal, die Bar und das Restaurant sind miteinander verbunden – damit wird der Blick aufs Wasser von Jazz begleitet.

CLUBS, LOUNGES +BARS

ESCAPE

Rembrandtplein 11 // Centrum
Tel.: +31 (0)20 6 22 11 11
www.escape.nl

Thu 11 pm to 4 am
Fri–Sat to 5 am
Sun to 4.30 am

Tram 4, 9, 14 Rembrandtplein

Prices: $$$

MAP N° **41**

Established 25 years ago, Escape is one of the oldest clubs in the city and an institution in Amsterdam's nightlife. Opened initially as a classic disco, Escape on the Rembrandtplein was expanded several times over the years and is now a mixture of café, restaurant, lounge bar, studio, and cool club with the best sounds, light installations, and visuals. On the weekends, DJs, LJs, and VJs present a wide variety of events on two dance floors.

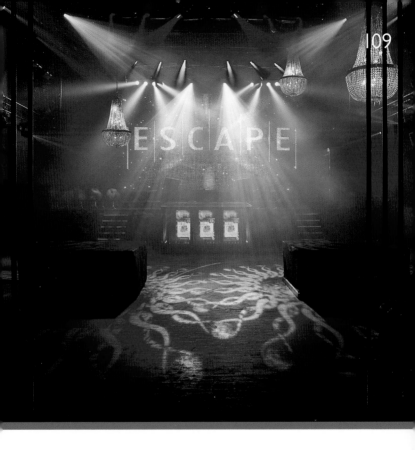

Das Escape gehört mit nunmehr 25 Jahren zu den ältesten Clubs der Stadt und gilt als eine Institution im Amsterdamer Nachtleben. Zunächst eine klassische Disco, wurde das Escape am Rembrandtplein regelmäßig erweitert und präsentiert sich heute als eine Mischung aus Café, Restaurant, Lounge-bar, Studio und coolem Club mit den besten Sounds, Lichtinstallationen und Visuals. DJs, LJs und VJs garantieren am Wochenende abwechslungsreiche Events auf zwei Dancefloors.

JIMMY WOO

JIMMY WOO

Korte Leidsedwarsstraat 18
Centrum
Tel.: +31 (0)20 6 26 31 50
www.jimmywoo.nl

Thu 11 pm to 3 am
Fri–Sun 11 pm to 4 am

Tram 1, 2, 5, 7, 10 Leidseplein

Prices: $$$

A popular club frequented by Dutch celebrities, Jimmy Woo hosts weekly club nights and events. Under the sparkling ceilings, DJs rev up a mixed crowd on the dance floor. If you prefer a quieter spot or simply want to take a breather, you can slip away to the exclusive lounge on the upper level where soft couches and small, round tables are reminiscent of a classic nightclub.

Ein Club, der gerne von nationaler Prominenz frequentiert wird. Im Jimmy Woo finden wöchentlich Clubnights und Events statt. Unter den glitzernden Decken heizen DJs dem gemischten Publikum auf dem Dancefloor ein. Wer es ruhiger haben oder eine Verschnaufpause einlegen möchte, der kann sich im Obergeschoss in die exklusive Lounge zurückziehen, wo weiche Sofas und kleine, runde Tische an einen klassischen Nachtclub erinnern.

MAP N° 42

The golden Buddha statue in the trendy lounge bar exudes calm and serenity. The peaceful Far Eastern atmosphere is underscored by sushi menus and the chill-out music that has found international success as the sound of the Buddha Bar. Little Buddha may be the little sister of the Paris bar bearing the same name, but this Amsterdam lounge bar is anything but small: It is one of the city's largest clubs and is located directly on the Leidseplein, a perfect spot for night owls.

LITTLE BUDDHA

Kleine Gartmanplantsoen 17
Centrum
Tel.: +31 (0)20 5 30 71 21
www.littlebuddhaamsterdam.com

Daily 5 pm to 1 am
Fri–Sat to 2 am

Tram 1, 2, 5, 7, 10 Leidseplein

Prices: $$$

MAP N° **43**

Ruhe und Gelassenheit strahlt die goldene Buddhastatue in der trendigen Loungebar aus. Die friedliche fernöstliche Atmosphäre wird von Sushi-Menüs und Chill-out-Musik, die als Sound der Buddha-Bar international erfolgreich ist, unterstrichen. Little Buddha ist die kleine Schwester der gleichnamigen Bar in Paris. Klein ist die Amsterdamer Loungebar aber keineswegs, im Gegenteil: Sie ist einer der größten Clubs und liegt für Nachtschwärmer günstig direkt am Leidseplein.

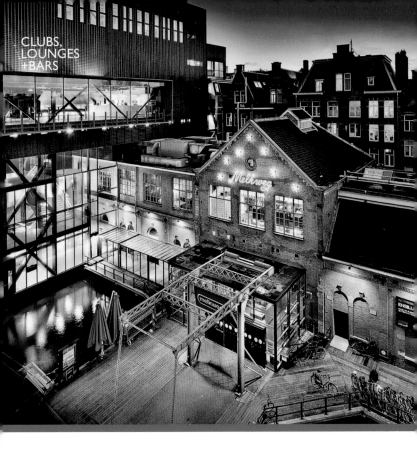

This legendary temple to pop music opened in 1970 in a former milk factory in the city center and made headlines as a hangout for the hippie scene. Despite the changing spirit of the times and several renovations, Melkweg has retained its industrial look and its special creative atmosphere. For an entertaining evening, the venue offers a theater, movie theater, galleries, a café restaurant, and a tea room, but live performances are what truly set the right mood.

MELKWEG

Lijnbaansgracht 234a // Centrum
Tel.: +31 (0)20 5 31 81 81
www.melkweg.nl

Daily from 1 pm
(look at the programs)

Tram 1, 2, 5, 7, 10 Leidseplein

Prices: $

MAP N° 44

Der legendäre Popmusiktempel entstand 1970 in einer ehemaligen
Milchfabrik im Stadtzentrum und machte Schlagzeilen als Hang-out
für die Hippieszene. Trotz wechselnden Zeitgeists und Renovierungen
sind der industrielle Look sowie die besondere kreative Atmosphäre
erhalten geblieben. Für einen unterhaltsamen Abend stehen Theater,
Kino, Galerien, ein Café-Restaurant sowie ein Tearoom bereit, aber die
Liveauftritte sorgen erst für die richtige Stimmung.

CLUBS,
LOUNGES
+BARS

PAPENEILAND

Prinsengracht 2 // Centrum
Tel.: +31 (0)20 6 24 19 89
www.papeneiland.nl

Daily from 9 am

Tram 1, 2, 4, 5, 9, 16, 17, 24, 25, 26
Centraal Station

Prices: $

Amsterdam natives love going to cafés, but not necessarily to drink coffee.
A café is actually a pub where you can drink a beer, read the newspaper,
and meet with friends or colleagues. Instead of contemporary design,
cafés feature nostalgic décor with plenty of wood. "Bruine cafés" are
perfect examples of this: smoky pubs like Café Papeneiland, an institution
in Amsterdam with a fantastic location along two canals. Cheers!

Amsterdamer gehen gern ins Café, aber nicht auf einen Kaffee. Ein
Café ist eigentlich eine urige Kneipe. Man trinkt hier sein Bier, liest die
Zeitung oder trifft sich mit Freunden oder Kollegen. Im Café gibt es
kein modernes Design, sondern nostalgische Einrichtung mit viel Holz.
Beispielhaft sind sogenannte „Bruine Cafés": verrauchte Kneipen wie
das Café Papeneiland, eine Institution in Amsterdam in toller Lage an
zwei Grachten. Prost!

SKY LOUNGE

CLUBS,
LOUNGES
+BARS

SKY LOUNGE

Oosterdoksstraat 4 // Centrum
Tel.: +31 (0)20 5 30 08 00
www.amsterdam.doubletree.com

Daily 11 am to 1 am, Fri–Sat to 3 am

Tram 1, 2, 4, 5, 9, 16, 17, 24, 25, 26
Centraal Station
Metro 51, 53, 54 Centraal Station

Prices: $$$$

MAP N° **46**

A new sky bar recently opened in Amsterdam: the Sky Lounge on the
11th floor of the Double Tree Hotel by Hilton Amsterdam Centraal
Station. You can take in spectacular 360-degree views of the city: from
the historic gables and church towers in the city center to the modern
architecture at the old harbor to the Noord district. The interior
design combines peaceful whites and warm shades of red with wood
and glass. Small dishes can be ordered in addition to drinks.

Amsterdam ist seit Kurzem um eine neue Skybar reicher: die Sky Lounge im 11. Stockwerk des Double Tree Hotel by Hilton Amsterdam Centraal Station. Von dort oben eröffnet sich ein 360-Grad-Ausblick über die Stadt: von den historischen Giebeln und Kirchtürmen im Zentrum über moderne Architektur am alten Hafen bis hin zum Stadtteil Noord. Bei der Einrichtung wurden ruhiges Weiß und warme Rottöne mit Holz und Glas kombiniert. Neben Getränken werden auch kleine Gerichte angeboten.

NOORDERLICHT

NDSM Plein 102 // Noord
Tel.: +31 (0)20 4 92 27 70
www.noorderlichtcafe.nl

Daily from 11 am
(closed on Mon in autumn and winter)

Ferry boat 903, 906 NDSM-werf
Bus 35 Atatürk
Bus 38, 94 Klaprozenweg

Prices: $

MAP N° **47**

Squatting is passé. New construction projects have displaced the alternative scene. New spaces have sprung up in the city district slowly emerging on the northern bank of the IJ. One of the meeting places for the creative and art-loving crowd is Café Noorderlicht on the old factory grounds of the NDSM shipyard. Artists are free to experiment near the former docks and in the halls, and there's often a great party atmosphere. Menus that change daily offer memorable culinary experiences.

Häuser besetzen ist passé. Die alternative Szene wurde von Neubauprojekten verdrängt. Neuer Raum entstand im langsam aufstrebenden Stadtgebiet am nördlichen IJ-Ufer. Einer der Treffpunkte kreativer und kunstsinniger Geister ist das Café Noorderlicht auf dem alten Fabrikgelände der Schiffswerft NDSM. Bei den ehemaligen Docks und in den Hallen darf experimentiert werden und es herrscht oft gute Partystimmung. Wechselnde Tagesmenüs sorgen für kulinarische Erlebnisse.

CANVAS OP DE 7DE

A lounge now occupies the spot where daily newspapers once ran off the printing press. Canvas has opened its doors in the former cafeteria on the 7th floor of the old "Volkskrant" building. The panoramic terrace, once reserved for newspaper staff, is a new hot spot in Amsterdam. From the inside, lounge music spills out onto the terrace, the mood is relaxed, the crowd is mixed, and the sunsets are spectacular. Canvas offers a short food menu, a long drinks menu, and a wide variety of events on weekends.

CANVAS OP DE 7^{DE}

Wibautstraat 150 // Oost
Tel.: +31 (0)20 7 16 38 17
www.canvas7.nl

Daily 11 am to 1 am
Fri, Sat to 3 am

Tram 3 Wibautstraat
Bus 355 Wibautstraat
Metro 51, 53, 54 Wibautstraat

Prices: $

MAP N°

Wo einst Tageszeitungen aus der Druckerpresse liefen, befindet sich heute eine Lounge. Im 7. Stock des alten „Volkskrant"-Gebäudes, in der ehemaligen Kantine, öffnete Canvas seine Pforten. Die Panoramaterrasse, früher dem Zeitungspersonal vorbehalten, ist nun ein neuer Hotspot in der Stadt. Von innen dringt Loungemusik heraus, die Stimmung ist entspannt, das Publikum gemischt, die Sonnenuntergänge sind traumhaft. Canvas bietet eine kurze Menükarte, eine lange Getränkekarte und jede Menge Events am Wochenende.

CLUBS,
LOUNGES
+BARS

TONIGHT

's-Gravesandestraat 51 // Oost
Tel.: +31 (0)20 8 50 24 00
www.hotelarena.nl

Fri–Sun 7 pm to 4 am

Tram 7, 10 Korte 's-Gravesandestraat
Tram 3 Beukenweg

Prices: $$

MAP N° 49

Celebrate in style until the early morning hours—where else can you find a dance floor where you can gaze up into a church dome painted with frescoes? Tonight is part of the Hotel Arena, once a Catholic orphanage from the 19th century. Today it is a multifunctional complex that blends history with Dutch design. The club consists of the Kerkzaal in the old chapel with different corners devoted to dancing and relaxing as well as the garden room adjacent to the terrace.

Feiern bis in die Morgenstunden und dazu in Style – wo sonst überspannt eine Kirchenkuppel mit Fresken den Dancefloor? Das Tonight ist Teil des Hotels Arena, einst ein katholisches Waisenhaus aus dem 19. Jahrhundert, heute ein multifunktionaler Komplex, wo Geschichte und holländisches Design kombiniert werden. Der Club besteht aus dem Kerkzaal in der alten Kapelle mit verschiedenen Ecken zum Tanzen und Entspannen und dem an die Terrasse anschließenden Gartensaal.

Momo, a trendy spot bordering the stylish Museumkwartier and the dynamic Leidseplein, is a popular meeting place for cool and beautiful Amsterdam natives. The name comes from the Japanese and means "flowering" and "beauty"; this is reflected in the modern design and the warm ambience. Momo offers fusion cuisine and exquisite drinks. The cocktails are seductive; according to one award, they make Momo one of the best cocktail bars in Amsterdam.

MOMO

Hobbemastraat 1 // Zuid
Tel.: +31 (0)20 6 71 74 74
www.momo-amsterdam.com

Bar: daily 10 am to 1 am
Fri–Sat to 2 am
Lunch, Dinner: daily noon to 11 pm
Sun to 10 pm, Mon–Wed to 10.30 pm

Tram 2, 5 Hobbemastraat
Tram 1 Stadhouderskade
Bus 358 Hobbemastraat

Prices: $$$

MAP N° 50

Amsterdams Coole und Schöne treffen sich gerne im trendigen Momo an
der Grenze des schicken Museumkwartier zum dynamischen Leidseplein.
Der Name stammt aus dem Japanischen, bedeutet Blüte und Schönheit
und spiegelt sich im modernen Design und der warmen Ausstrahlung wider.
Geboten werden Gerichte aus der Fusionsküche und exquisite Getränke.
Verführerisch sind die Cocktails, mit denen das Momo laut einer
Auszeichnung zu den besten Cocktailbars Amsterdams zählt.

The name speaks for itself: The bar is located on the 23rd floor of the luxurious Hotel Okura. You can hardly get any higher for a panoramic view over the rooftops of Amsterdam. Relax on dark leather stools and wind up the evening over a cocktail, an exquisite glass of wine, or a glass of champagne while taking in the unobstructed view of the city lights. You can also nibble on tidbits from the award-winning Ciel Bleu Restaurant right next door. The Twenty Third Bar places a high value on quality and service.

TWENTY THIRD

Ferdinand Bolstraat 333 // Zuid
Tel.: +31 (0)20 6 78 71 11
www.okura.nl

Daily 6 pm to 1 am, Fri–Sat to 2 am

Tram 25 Cornelis Troostplein

Prices: $$$$

MAP N° 51

Der Name spricht für sich: Die Bar befindet sich im 23. Stock des Luxushotels Okura. Höher geht es kaum noch für einen Panoramablick über die Amsterdamer Dächer. Auf dunklen Lederstühlen lässt man bei einem Cocktail, einem erlesenen Wein oder einem Gläschen Champagner den Abend ausklingen, mit freiem Blick auf das Lichtermeer der Stadt. Dazu ein Häppchen aus dem angrenzenden preisgekrönten Restaurant Ciel Bleu. Im Twenty Third wird Wert auf Qualität und Service gelegt.

HIGHLIGHTS

AMSTEL

Centrum

Metro 51, 53, 54 Waterlooplein
Tram 9, 14 Muntplein
or Waterlooplein
Tram 16, 24, 25 Muntplein

MAP N° 52

On your first visit to Amsterdam, there's one thing you must experience: a boat trip through the canals. You will pass by historic canal houses, different houseboats, and under countless bridges on your way up the Amstel, the river that gave Amsterdam its name. Barges still occasionally use the river, and when they do the locks open and drawbridges lift, including the Magere Brug, or "skinny bridge." Even Amsterdam natives pause to witness this rare show.

Wer Amsterdam zum ersten Mal besucht, kommt nicht drum herum:
eine Bootsfahrt durch die Grachten. Vorbei an historischen Grachtenhäusern,
unter unzähligen Brücken hindurch und entlang unterschiedlicher
Hausboote geht es hinaus auf die Amstel, die Namensgeberin der Stadt.
Ab und an wird der Fluss noch von Lastkähnen benutzt. Dann öffnen sich
die Schleusen und klappen die Brücken hoch, sogar die Magere Brug. Um
dieses seltene Schauspiel zu sehen, halten selbst noch die Amsterdamer an.

BEGIJNHOF

Spui // Centrum
Tel.: +31 (0)20 6 22 19 18
www.begijnhofamsterdam.nl

Daily 9 am to 5 pm

Tram 1, 2, 4, 5, 9, 16, 24, 25 Spui

MAP N°

The inner courtyards, often concealed behind nondescript doors along the canals, are called "Hofjes." Peaceful, green oases surrounded by idyllic houses, most of these courtyards are very old and were constructed primarily for single women. Perhaps the best-known courtyard, Begijnhof also boasts the oldest house in the city. It retains its intimate atmosphere in spite of its numerous visitors. And the residents? The Begijnhof is still home to women only!

„Hofjes" nennt man die Innenhöfe, die sich häufig hinter unscheinbaren Türen an den Grachten verstecken. Es sind Oasen der Ruhe, umringt von idyllischen Häusern und immer begrünt. Die meisten Höfe sind sehr alt und wurden primär für alleinstehende Frauen gebaut. Der Begijnhof ist wohl der bekannteste und beherbergt zudem das älteste Haus der Stadt. Trotz der vielen Besucher ist die intime Atmosphäre erhalten geblieben. Und die Bewohner? Im Begijnhof leben immer noch nur Frauen!

At some point, every tourist passes by the Dam. The city's history began here, and Amsterdam has this historic square to thank for part of its name. The square has several striking features: the National Monument, where visitors enjoy relaxing, and the Royal Palace, which was originally designed as the city hall and is now at the disposal of the royal family and their guests. Some of the magnificent rooms have been renovated and are now open to the public—they are well worth a visit.

DE DAM

Centrum

Tram 4, 9, 16, 24, 25 Dam

MAP N°

Am Dam kommt jeder Tourist irgendwann mal vorbei. Die Stadtgeschichte begann hier und dem historischen Platz hat Amsterdam auch einen Teil seines Namens zu verdanken. Als Blickfang dienen das Nationalmonument, an dem man gerne die Füße ausstreckt, und der königliche Palast, der als Rathaus konzipiert war und heute dem Königshaus und dessen Gästen zur Verfügung steht. Einige der renovierten Prunkräume sind auch der Öffentlichkeit zugänglich und lohnen eine Besichtigung.

DE JORDAAN

DE JORDAAN

Centrum

Tram 3 Marnixplein
Tram 10 Bloemgracht or Marnixplein
Tram 13, 14, 17 Rozengracht
or Westermarkt

MAP N° 55

Once a working-class district west of Prinsengracht, this lively district full of creativity and contrasts has become a sought-after residential area over the years. With its mixture of young and old, businesses and galleries, cafés and trendy restaurants, the Jordaan district has its own flair, a blend of both traditional and sophisticated elements. The easiest way to explore Jordaan is by bicycle—how could it be any other way in Amsterdam?

Aus dem ehemaligen Arbeiterviertel westlich der Prinsengracht ist
heute eine begehrte Wohngegend geworden, ein lebendiger Bezirk
voller Kreativität und Kontraste. Der Jordaan bietet durch seinen Mix
aus Alt und Jung, Geschäften und Galerien, Cafés und Szenerestaurants
ein eigenes Flair, volkstümlich und mondän zugleich. Eine Entdeckungstour
durch den Jordaan lässt sich am einfachsten, wie könnte es in Amsterdam
auch anders sein, mit dem Rad unternehmen.

The Hermitage Amsterdam is a dependency of the Hermitage Museum of Saint Petersburg. The historic tie between the two cities can be traced back to Russian Czar Peter the Great's visit to Holland. The Hermitage Amsterdam is beautifully located on the eastern bank of the river Amstel. Housed in a former nursing home, following an extensive renovation the museum now offers changing exhibitions, regular concerts, and an excellent restaurant in the interior courtyard.

HERMITAGE

Amstel 51 // Centrum
Tel.: +31 (900) 4 37 64 82 43
www.hermitage.nl

Daily 10 am to 5 pm
Wed to 8 pm

Metro 51, 53, 54 Waterlooplein
Tram 9, 14 Waterlooplein

MAP N° 56

Die Hermitage in Amsterdam ist eine Zweigstelle des gleichnamigen Museums in Sankt Petersburg. Das historische Band zwischen den Städten ist auf den Aufenthalt des Zaren Peters des Großen in Holland zurückzuführen. Die Hermitage liegt wunderschön am rechten Amstelufer. Sie ist in einem ehemaligen Altersheim untergebracht und bietet nach einem großen Umbau wechselnde Ausstellungen, regelmäßige Konzerte und ein gutes Restaurant im Innenhof.

HIGHLIGHTS

Centrum

Tram 1, 2, 5, 7, 10 Leidseplein
Tram 9, 14 Rembrandtplein

With wicker chairs and tables lined up in front of cafés, terraces fill quickly once the first rays of spring sunshine can be felt. Everyone enjoys soaking up the sun, meeting for a cool drink, and watching the hustle and bustle in the square. At Rembrandtplein and Leidseplein squares, both of which are entertainment hotspots, there's always something going on around the clock. These two squares magically draw everyone: tourists, natives, street musicians, night owls, and young and old alike.

Die Korbstühle und Tische stehen in Reih und Glied vor den Cafés. Mit den ersten Sonnenstrahlen im Frühling füllen sich die Terrassen schnell. Man genießt die warme Sonne, trifft sich zu einem kühlen Drink und beobachtet das Treiben auf dem Platz. Am Rembrandtplein und am Leidseplein, den beiden Vergnügungsstätten schlechthin, ist immer etwas los, und das rund um die Uhr. Touristen, Einheimische, Straßenmusikanten, Nachtschwärmer, Jung und Alt – alle zieht es magisch zu diesen Hotspots.

Centrum

Metro 51, 53, 54 Waterlooplein
Tram 9, 14 Waterlooplein

Waterlooplein hosts what is perhaps the best-known flea market in the city, a tradition that can be traced back to the 19th century. Visitors looking for bargains can rummage through art and kitsch as well as new, used, contemporary, and old fashioned items. There are no set prices, and haggling is expected. The flea market shares the square with the Stopera, a building complex that houses the town hall with the Amsterdam Ordnance Datum and the city's opera house.

Der Name Waterlooplein steht für den wohl bekanntesten Flohmarkt der Stadt. Der Markt hat Tradition, seine Geschichte geht bis ins 19. Jahrhundert zurück. Die Besucher stöbern zwischen Kunst und Kitsch, zwischen Neu und Gebraucht, zwischen Modern und Altmodisch nach Schnäppchen. Die Preise sind nicht festgelegt, Handeln ist erlaubt. Der Flohmarkt teilt sich den Platz mit dem Stopera, einem Gebäude-komplex, in dem das Rathaus mit dem Amsterdamer Pegel und ein Musiktheater untergebracht sind.

STADSEILANDEN

2

Centrum and Oost

Tram 26, Bus 48 Jan Schaeferbrug (Java-eiland)
Tram 10, Bus 48, 65, 359 Azartplein (KNSM-eiland)
Tram 10, Bus 48, 65, 359 C. van Eesterenlaan (Sporenbrug)
Bus 48, 359 Bornelaan (Borneo-eiland)

In the Eastern Docklands, Amsterdam has completely reinvented itself. Warehouses, cranes, and sheds once located on the docks and harbor islands have had to make way for an inspiring and unique style of waterfront architecture. The old scene of squatters, artists, and students is now a thing of the past. Dynamic and successful urbanites in particular now reside in the hip and highly coveted city districts of Sporenbrug, and Java, KNSM, and Borneo islands.

Amsterdam erfand sich völlig neu im östlichen Hafengebiet. Auf den ehemaligen Kais und Hafeninseln mussten die Speicher, Verladekräne und Schuppen einer inspirierenden und eigenwilligen Architektur am Wasser weichen. Die alte Szene von Hausbesetzern, Künstlern und Studenten gehört längst der Vergangenheit an. Heute leben in den hippen und heiß begehrten Stadtteilen Sporenbrug, Java-, KNSM- und Borneo-eiland vor allem dynamische und erfolgreiche Großstädter.

RED LIGHT DISTRICT

Centrum, Burgwallen

Metro 51, 53, 54 Nieuwmarkt
Tram 4, 9, 16, 24, 25 Dam

MAP N° 60

For many tourists, an evening walk through Amsterdam's red light district is a standard feature of a city tour. They want to see for themselves the lingerie-clad women offering their services behind shop windows. Red lights on the buildings confirm the special image of this city district. Referred to as De Wallen by locals, this area is a labyrinth of canals, bridges, and narrow lanes in the historic city center. This district is not just for loose women.

Ein Abendspaziergang durch das Rotlichtviertel gehört für viele Besucher zum Standardprogramm einer Stadtbesichtigung. Mit eigenen Augen wollen sie es sehen: Frauen in Dessous, die hinter den Schaufenstern ihre Dienste anbieten. Rote Lampen an den Gebäuden bestätigen das spezielle Image dieses Stadtteils. De Wallen, wie die Amsterdamer das Gebiet nennen, ist ein Labyrinth von Grachten, Stegen und Gassen im historischen Stadtkern. Ein Bezirk nicht nur für leichte Mädchen.

HERENGRACHT AND KEIZERSGRACHT

Centrum, Grachtengordel

Tram 13, 14, 17 Westermarkt
Tram 1, 2, 4, 5, 7, 10, 16, 24, 25
Keizersgracht

MAP N° 61

Anywhere you go in the city center, you'll encounter water. Amsterdam has countless canals. The Herengracht and the Keizersgracht are two exquisitely beautiful canals that surround the city center like a belt. As in the past, these canals are still the city's most exclusive and expensive residential areas. In the 17th century, only the wealthiest merchants could afford to settle here, and their gabled houses were a direct reflection of their business success—ideally wider and more impressive than the neighboring house.

Wo man im Zentrum auch geht und steht, man stößt immer auf
Wasser. Amsterdam hat unzählige Kanäle. Die Herengracht und die
Keizersgracht, die sich wie ein Gürtel um das Zentrum legen, sind
die schönsten und stehen heute für die besten und teuersten Adressen
der Stadt, wie schon im 17. Jahrhundert. Nur die reichsten Kaufleute
konnten sich hier niederlassen und sie zeigten ihren kaufmännischen
Erfolg mit Giebelhäusern – am besten breiter und imposanter als
das Nachbarhaus.

HIGHLIGHTS

MUSEUM
VAN LOON

Keizersgracht 672 // Centrum, Grachtengordel
Tel.: +31 (0)20 6 24 52 55
www.museumvanloon.nl

Wed–Mon 11 am to 5 pm
The coach house is opened every hour for 15 minutes
by museum staff at 11.30 am, 12.30 pm, 1 pm, 2.30 pm,
3.30 pm and 4.30 pm

Tram 16, 24, 25 Keizersgracht

The Museum Van Loon offers curious visitors a look at what life was like in the elegant living and working spaces concealed behind the façade of a historic canal house. The museum breathes the wealth and atmosphere of the 17th century and features period furniture, silver and porcelain tableware, and portraits of the former residents. The backyard surprises visitors with a beautiful garden, and the former Koetshuis (coach house) hosts regular art exhibitions.

Neugierig auf das Leben hinter der Fassade eines Grachtenhauses? Das Museum Van Loon bietet die Möglichkeit, einen Blick in elegante historische Wohn- und Arbeitsräume zu werfen. Das Haus atmet den Reichtum und die Atmosphäre des 17. Jahrhunderts: Stilmöbel, Tafelgeschirr aus Silber und Porzellan und Porträts der einstigen Bewohner. Im Hinterhof überrascht ein schöner Garten und im ehemaligen Koetshuis (Wagenburg) finden regelmäßig Kunstausstellungen statt.

PRINSENGRACHT

Amsterdam's favorite place to celebrate is on the water. Prinsengracht canal has proven to be quite the party area. Every year on April 30th, the day the Queen's birthday is officially celebrated, the canal is decorated in orange, the color of the royal house. During the Gay Pride Canal Parade, pink sets the tone. In August, the atmosphere is more contemplative for the classical Prinsengracht concert held on a floating stage. And when the water freezes, the canal transforms itself into an ice skating paradise.

PRINSENGRACHT

Centrum, Grachtengordel

Tram 13, 14, 17 Westermarkt
Tram 1, 2, 4, 5, 7, 10, 16, 24, 25
Prinsengracht

MAP N° 63

Wenn Amsterdam feiert, dann am liebsten auf dem Wasser. Die
Prinsengracht wurde als Partymeile ausgewiesen. Jährlich am 30. April,
an dem der Geburtstag der Königin offiziell gefeiert wird, färbt sich die
Gracht in Orange, der Farbe des Königshauses. Während der Canal
Parade (Gay Pride) beherrscht Rosa das Geschehen. Beschaulicher
ist es im August, wenn auf einer schwimmenden Bühne das klassische
Prinsengracht-Konzert abgehalten wird. Und wenn es mal friert,
verwandelt sich die Gracht in ein Eislaufparadies.

Amsterdam has always exerted a powerful attraction, especially to artists and other creative minds. Rembrandt was 29 years old when he moved to Amsterdam, the city where he celebrated his greatest successes. He lived and worked for almost 20 years behind the green door and the red windows of this striking gabled house. Now a museum, visitors can wander through various rooms and Rembrandt's studio to admire his numerous etchings and engravings on display alongside 17th-century furniture.

MUSEUM HET REMBRANDTHUIS

Jodenbreestraat 4
Centrum, Nieuwmarkt
Tel.: +31 (0)20 5 20 04 00
www.rembrandthuis.nl

Daily 10 am to 5 pm

Metro 50, 54 Waterlooplein

MAP N°

Amsterdam übte schon immer eine große Anziehungskraft aus, insbesondere auf Künstler und andere kreative Geister. Rembrandt war 29 Jahre alt, als er nach Amsterdam zog, wo er seine größten Erfolge feierte. Hinter der grünen Tür und den roten Fenstern des auffallenden Giebelhauses lebte und arbeitete er fast 20 Jahre lang. In verschiedenen Wohnräumen und in seinem Atelier, zwischen Möbeln aus dem 17. Jahrhundert, werden zahlreiche Radierungen und Stiche des Meisters gezeigt.

DE PIJP

Zuid

Tram 10, 24 Stadhouderskade or
Albert Cuypstraat
Tram 3,12, 25 Ferdinand Bolstraat

MAP N° 65

Amsterdam is more than just canals and gabled houses. De Pijp is the
residential "place to be" outside of the historic center. This part of
the city is dynamic and multicultural thanks to its large student population.
Located in the center of the action, the Albert Cuyp Market is reputedly
the largest daytime market in Europe. Its clientele is international and
just as diverse as the range of products sold there. De Pijp is at its best
on a sunny day when terraces in small, sleepy courtyards provide
inviting spots to linger.

Amsterdam ist mehr als nur Grachten und Giebelhäuser. „The place to be" außerhalb des historischen Zentrums ist das Wohnviertel De Pijp. Dieser Teil der Stadt gilt als studentisch, dynamisch und multikulturell. Inmitten des Geschehens erstreckt sich der Albert-Cuyp-Markt, gerühmt als längster Markt Europas. Sein Publikum ist international und genauso vielfältig ist sein Warenangebot. De Pijp zeigt sich von seiner besten Seite, wenn die Sonne scheint. Dann laden die Terrassen auf den kleinen, verschlafenen Plätzen zum Verweilen ein.

VAN-GOGH-MUSEUM

Paulus Potterstraat 7
Zuid, Museumkwartier
Tel.: +31 (0)20 5 70 52 00
www.vangoghmuseum.nl

Daily 10 am to 6 pm, Fri to 10 pm

Tram 2, 5 Van Baerlestraat

MAP N° 66

Although his style was scarcely appreciated during his lifetime, today the works of Vincent van Gogh draw countless visitors to Amsterdam. Nowhere else on earth can you find so many of his paintings under one roof as in the capital of the Netherlands. The Van Gogh Museum exhibits many of this genius' paintings, including "The Potato Eaters" from his early, dark phase, his self portraits from his time in Paris, and his famous sunflower paintings from his time in Provence.

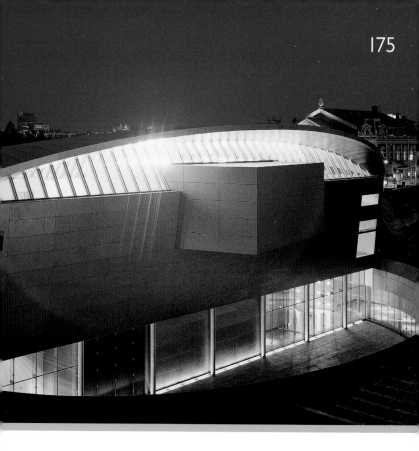

Sein Stil fand zu Lebzeiten kaum Anerkennung, heute locken die Werke des Malergenies Vincent van Gogh unzählige Besucher nach Amsterdam. Nirgendwo sonst auf der Welt sind so viele seiner Gemälde unter einem Dach zu bewundern wie in der niederländischen Hauptstadt. Die „Kartoffelesser" aus seiner dunklen Frühphase, die Selbstporträts aus seiner Zeit in Paris oder die weltberühmten „Sonnenblumen" aus der Provence sind nur einige der Gemälde, die das Museum ausstellt.

VONDELPARK

Stadhouderskade
Zuid, Museumkwartier

Daily 8 am to 7 pm

Tram 1 Stadhouderskade
(Main entrance) or J. P. Heijestraat

MAP N° 67

If you want to soak up some fresh air and find a quiet place to escape the big city noise for a few minutes, Vondelpark, Amsterdam's most beloved park, is located just a few steps away from Leidseplein, a popular nightlife area. In the 1960s, hippies slept undisturbed on the park's grassy expanses. Amsterdam has always enjoyed a more laid-back lifestyle. Today, Vondelpark attests to the ease and the multicultural character of the Dutch capital.

Frische Luft tanken, Ruhe suchen, dem Großstadtlärm für ein paar Minuten entfliehen – nur wenige Schritte vom beliebten Ausgehviertel Leidseplein ist das möglich. Denn dort erstreckt sich Amsterdams beliebtester Park, der Vondelpark. Auf seinem Rasen schliefen in den 1960er Jahren ungestört die Hippies. Amsterdam nahm und nimmt das Leben eben lockerer. Heute bezeugt der Vondelpark die Leichtigkeit und den multikulturellen Charakter der niederländischen Hauptstadt.

COOL
DISTRICTS

CENTRUM
Designated a World Heritage Site in 2010, the historic center within the ring of canals is the heart of the city. A popular residential area for shopping and going out; the canal houses are considered prestigious addresses.

DE JORDAAN
A historic district with a labyrinth of alleys, bridges, and canals. De Jordaan stands for fashion, design, and art, as well as pubs with a good atmosphere. It is a favorite of hip crowds and Amsterdam natives alike.

DE PIJP
It feels as if the entire world is represented in this cosmopolitan district. A favorite residential area for young and old alike with shopping at the large Albert Cuyp Market and trendy lounge cafés and restaurants where you can eat and drink.

MUSEUMKWARTIER
Exclusive residential area surrounding the Van Gogh Museum, the Rijksmuseum, and the Concertgebouw, with Vondelpark just steps away. P. C. Hoofdstraat is famous throughout Holland—a chic shopping street and the place to see and be seen.

NOORD
An up-and-coming working-class district and waterfront area separated from the rest of the city by the IJ but which is easily accessible thanks to free ferry connections. Old factories and shipyards along the shoreline are being transformed into new urban hot spots.

OOSTELIJK HAVENGEBIED
The former docks are scarcely recognizable since their metamorphosis into a modern residential area. In this area, people live on the water in luxury apartments with a panoramic view or row houses with a jetty. The city harbor is now a destination for cruise ships. Cool clubs and restaurants have sprung up around the terminal.

WESTERPARK
The district is experiencing an upturn since the Westergasfabriek was renovated. The old factory building in the city park offers room for art and culture, relaxed cafés and restaurants. A good place to relax in the middle of the city and a favorite spot on weekends for parents with young children.

ZUID
Apart from the Museumkwartier and De Pijp, Zuid has other coveted residential areas. On the edge of the district are the exhibition grounds, where Zuidas has emerged and become a prestigious location for modern architecture and international companies.

ZUIDOOST
A multicultural city district that emerged in the 1960s based on plans by Le Corbusier and which continues to develop step by step today. The Ajax Arena and two new concert halls are located in this district.

COOL
MAP

JAVA-EILAND 59

COOL
MAP

21

20

36

40

46

PIET HEINKADE

12

**NIEUWMARKT
EN LASTAGE**

HENDRIKKADE

IJTUNNEL

KATTENBURGERSTRAAT

PANAMALAAN

**OOSTELIJKE
EILANDEN
EN KADIJKEN**

ALKENBURGER

OOSTENBURGERGRACHT

CRUQUIUS

**OOSTELIJK
HAVENGEBIED**

**HORTUS
BOTANICUS
AMSTERDAM**

PLANTAGE MIDDENLAAN

ZEEBURGERDIJK

25

WEESPERSTRAAT

**WEESPERBUURT
EN PLANTAGE**

**INDISCHE
BUURT WEST**

DAPPERBUURT

49

WIJTTENBACHSTRAAT

7

MAURITSKADE

LINNAEUSSTRAAT

23

WIBAUTSTRAAT

BEUKENWEG

48

MIDDENWE

22

EMERGENCY

Emergency number for ambulance,
fire department, and police: 112

ARRIVAL

BY AIRPLANE

SCHIPHOL AIRPORT
Approximately 20 km/13 miles south of the
city center. National and international flights
between 5 am and noon. Up-to-date information
regarding flights and airport operations is
available in various languages at
www.schiphol.nl.

The train offers the best, fastest, and cheapest
way to travel into the city. Departures from
the lower level of the central hall (Schiphol
Plaza) every 10 minutes to the main train station
(Centraal Station); duration approximately
18 minutes. Up-to-date information regarding
trains is available at **www.ns.nl.**
Taxis are available outside of the arrival hall,
as are free hotel shuttle buses, particularly for
hotels in the immediate vicinity of the airport.

BY TRAIN

MAIN TRAIN STATION
The main train station (Centraal Station)
is located on the northern edge of the city
center and for tourists is the most important

train station in Amsterdam because all
national and international trains stop here.
The historic city center is just a few minutes
away on foot. From the main train station,
visitors can connect to public transportation
to every part of the city. Information about
public transportation is available at
www.gvb.nl.

TOURIST INFORMATION

AMSTERDAM TOURIST BOARD
Stationsplein 10
(across from Centraal Station)
Tel.: +31 (0)20 2 01 88 00
Daily 9 am to 5 pm
www.iamsterdam.com
Official tourist information website
for Amsterdam.

HOLLAND TOURIST INFORMATION
Schiphol Airport, Arrival Hall 2
Tel.: +31 (0)20 2 01 88 00
Daily 7 am to 10 pm
www.holland.com
Official tourist information website
for Holland.

ACCOMMODATIONS
www.iamsterdam.com
has links to different types of accommodation.
Hotels can also be found on websites
www.hotels.nl and **www.booking.nl.**

TICKETS AMSTERDAMS UITBURO (AUB)
Leidseplein 26
Mon–Fri noon to 7 pm, Sat, Sun to 6 pm
Stationsplein 10 (in the tourist information)
Daily noon to 5 pm (summer to 6 pm),
Fri, Sat to 6 pm
Oosterdokskade 143 (public library)
Mon–Fri noon to 7.30 pm, Sat, Sun to 6 pm
www.amsterdamsuitburo.nl

LAST MINUTE TICKETS
www.lastminuteticketshop.nl

AMSTERDAM CARD
Pay once and then travel free of charge on
the entire public transportation network for
24, 48, or 72 hours.
In addition, this card offers discounts and
free admission to nearly all museums.
**www.iamsterdam.com/nl/
visiting/iamsterdamcard**

GETTING AROUND

PUBLIC TRANSPORTATION
Up-to-date information about public
transportation in Amsterdam can be
found at **www.gvb.nl.**
For information by telephone,
call +31 (0)20 4 60 60 60.

TAXI

TAXI CENTRALE AMSTERDAM (TCA)
Tel.: +31 (0)20 7 77 77 77
www.tcataxi.nl

WATER TAXI
Tel.: +31 (0)20 5 35 63 63
www.water-taxi.nl

BIKE TAXI
Tel.: +31 (0)6 38 82 26 83
www.wielertaxi.nl

RICKSHAW PEDICAB TAXI
Tel.: +31 (0)6 47 26 83 16
www.amsterdambiketaxi.info

BICYCLE RENTAL

RENT A BIKE
Damstraat 20
Tel.: +31 (0)20 6 25 50 29
www.rentabike.nl

YELLOW BIKE
Nieuwezijds Kolk 29
Tel.: +31 (0)20 6 20 69 40
www.yellowbike.nl

ORANGE BIKE
Singel 233
Tel.: +31 (0)20 5 28 99 90
www.orangebike.nl

CITY BIKE
Bloemgracht 68–70
Tel.: +31 (0) 20 6 26 37 21 or 6 26 37 21
www.bikecity.nl

CAR RENTAL
Almost all car rental companies have an
office at Schiphol Airport.
www.hertz.nl
www.avis.nl
www.europcar.nl
www.nationalcar.nl
www.budget.nl
www.sixt.nl

CITY TOURS

INDIVIDUAL
The best way to explore the city center is
on foot, by bicycle (see BICYCLE RENTAL)
and/or by streetcar.
Tram 16 passes by the main attractions in
the city center. Up-to-date information can
be found at **www.gvb.nl**.
The Museum Cruise (**www.lovers.nl**) can
round out city center explorations.
A beautiful and fun alternative is a waterfiets
(pedal boat), which can be rented near the
Rijksmuseum (**www.canal.nl**).
A more exclusive way to explore the canals is
by private boat
(**www.classicboattours.nl**,
www.privateboattours.nl and
www.amsterdambyboat.nl).

ORGANIZED TOURS

BUS
The red hop-on, hop-off bus familiar
from other major cities now offers
service in Amsterdam.
www.citysightseeingamsterdam.nl

BOAT
Companies that offer canal tours
include the following:
www.blueboat.nl
www.canalcruiseamsterdam.nl
www.rederijkooij.nl www.dereddij.nl
www.canal.nl

TUKTUK
An unusual alternative to
organized bus and boat tours.
www.tuktuksightseeing.nl
www.tuktukuitjes.nl

GOING OUT
Information about "**What's happening in
Amsterdam**" is located on the tourist
information website
(**www.iamsterdam.com**),
in the Uitkrant monthly magazine
(**www.amsterdamsuitburo.nl/extra/uitkrant**),
and in the Amsterdam daily
newspaper "Het Parool"
(**www.parool.nl**).

EVENTS

JANUARY TO APRIL

AMSTERDAM FASHION WEEK
The fashion world focuses on Amsterdam in January and July when young Dutch fashion designers present their creations. **www.aifw.nl**

CHINESE NEW YEAR
Traditional dragon dance and spectacular fireworks displays take place in Nieuwmarkt square in historic Old Amsterdam.
www.iamsterdam.com/en/whats-on/ events/february/chinese-new-year

QUEEN'S DAY
Every year, the entire country celebrates the Queen's birthday on April 30th (a national holiday). The celebration is particularly exuberant with a great atmosphere in Amsterdam.
www.koninginnedagamsterdam.nl

MAY TO AUGUST

BEVRIJDINGSFESTIVAL
On May 5 (holiday), different music events revolving around freedom and peace are held throughout Amsterdam, particularly on Museumplein square.
www.bevrijdingsfestivals.nl

HOLLAND FESTIVAL
The month of June is all about the Holland Festival with numerous music, dance, theater, architecture, and visual arts performances and activities held at multiple locations throughout the city.
www.hollandfestival.nl

OPEN AIR THEATER
Free concerts and other events are held in the open air theater located in Vondelpark on Fridays through Sundays in the summertime.
ww.openluchttheater.nl

TASTE OF AMSTERDAM
Culinary festival held in Museumplein square in June featuring numerous restaurants whose chefs pamper visitors with delicacies.
www.tasteofamsterdam.com

AMSTERDAM ROOTS
Seven days of music, particularly from Africa and Latin America, in Oosterpark and in the most important pop temples of the city.
www.amsterdamroots.nl

JULIDANS
Internationally renowned festival for contemporary dance held in the Stadsschouwburg (municipal theater) on Leidseplein square.
www.julidans.nl

OVER HET IJ FESTIVAL
For eleven days, the buildings of the old shipyards in the Noord city district are transformed into stages for theatrical performances. **www.overhetij.nl**

INTERNATIONAL FASHION WEEK
(See January)

COOL
CITY INFO

CANAL PARADE
See and be seen is the motto of this large boat parade on the Prinsengracht canal, which started out as part of the annual gay pride festival. **www.canalparade.nl**

GRACHTENFESTIVAL
This festival features various classical concerts held on floating stages on the canals. The final concert is traditionally held on the Prinsengracht canal in front of the Hotel Pulitzer. **www.grachtenfestival.nl**

DE PARADE
Theater festival featuring music, dance, and cabaret performances at different locations throughout the city. **www.deparade.nl**

UITMARKT
Theaters introduce their program for the upcoming season. Free concerts and events on multiple stages in the city center.
www.uitmarkt.nl

KETI KOTI
Colorful festival on July 1 in Oosterpark to commemorate and celebrate the abolition of slavery.
www.ketikotiamsterdam.nl

SEPTEMBER TO DECEMBER

JORDAAN FESTIVAL
Ten day festival in the popular Jordaan city district with Dutch hit songs.
www.jordaanfestival.nl

OPEN MONUMENTENDAG (HERITAGE DAYS)
In early September, many historic buildings open their doors to the public. In addition, many museums offer free or discounted admission to coincide with the occasion.
www.openmonumentendag.nl

AMSTERDAM MARATHON
In October, the city welcomes long-distance runners from all over the world.
www.tcsamsterdammarathon.nl

MUSEUM NIGHT
Museum Night is held on the first weekend in November and features numerous events. Tickets are available only in advance.
www.n8.nl

IDFA
International film festival with around 200 documentaries from around the world.
www.idfa.nl

ART, ANTIQUITIES, AND DESIGN FAIR
Pan Amsterdam is the largest trade fair for art, antiquities, and design in Holland.
www.pan-amsterdam.nl

OUD EN NIEUW
New Year's Eve in Amsterdam is celebrated with plenty of music and fireworks. A free New Year's Eve party is held in Museumplein square featuring live performances by famous musicians.

COOL
CREDITS

Cover photo by El Nariz/Shutterstock Images
Back cover photos: Matthew Shaw; courtesy
Laura Dols; Hans Zaglitsch

pp. 2–3 (Technologiemuseum NEMO)
by Hans Zaglitsch
pp. 6–7 (Intro) by Hans Zaglitsch

HOTELS
pp. 10–11 (Esheréa) courtesy Hotel Estherea;
pp. 12–15 (Hotel V) courtesy Hotel V; pp.
16–19 (Pulitzer) courtesy Starwood Hotels;
pp. 20–21 (Seven One Seven) by Kees Hageman;
pp. 22–23 (The Grand) courtesy The Grand;
pp. 24–25 (The Times Hotel) courtesy The
Times Hotel; pp. 26–27 (Intercontinental Amstel
Amsterdam) courtesy InterContinental Amstel;
pp. 28–29 (De Filosoof) by Roland Bauer;
pp. 30–31 (Museum Suites) courtesy T. Capteln &
Museum Suites; pp. 32–33 (Park Hotel) courtesy
Park Hotel; pp. 34–35 (The College Hotel)
courtesy The College Hotel; pp 36–37 (Lloyd
Hotel) by Roland Bauer; pp. 38–39 (Qbic Hotel
Amsterdam) courtesy Qbic; pp. 40–41 (Zuiver)
p 41 top by Hans van de Vorst, all others by Karen
Steenwinkel

RESTAURANTS + CAFÉS
pp. 44–45 (Anna) courtesy Anna; pp. 46–47
(Bridges) courtesy The Bridges; pp. 48–49 (D'Vijff
Vlieghen) courtesy d'Vijff Vlieghen; pp. 50–51
(Lucius) courtesy Lucius; pp. 52–55 (Stanislavski)
courtesy Stanislavski; pp. 56–57 (Zouthaven)
courtesy Zouthaven; pp. 58–61 (Stork) by Seth
Carnill; pp. 62–63 (De Kas) p 62 by Ronald
Hoeben, all others by Jet van Fastenhout;
pp. 64–65 (De Ysbreeker) courtesy De Ysbreeker;
pp. 66–67 (Open) courtesy Open; pp. 68–71
(Pompstation) by Barwerd van der Plas;
pp. 72–73 (Visaandeschelde) by Leon Hendrickx,
www.leonhendrickx.com

SHOPS
pp. 76–77 (Bloemenmarkt) by Hans Zaglitsch;
pp. 78–79 (De Kaaskamer) by Hans Zaglitsch; pp.
80–81 (Floris van Bommel) by Monne Zwemmer/
Studio Senz; pp. 82–83 (Geels & Co) by Olaf Fokke;

pp. 84–85 (Jan Jansen) by Maurice Jansen; pp. 86–87
(Laura Dols) courtesy Laura Dols; pp. 88–89
(MagnaPlaza) by Hans Zaglitsch; pp. 90–91 (Mendo)
courtesy Mendo; pp. 92–93 (Nukuhiva) by
Humprey Daniels; pp. 94–95 (Thinking of Holland)
courtesy Thinking of Holland; pp. 96–97 (Unlimited
Delicious) by Hans Zaglitsch; pp. 98–99 (YDU) by
Hans Zaglitsch

CLUBS, LOUNGES + BARS
pp. 102–103 (Air Amsterdam) courtesy Air Amsterdam; pp. 104–107 (Bimhuis) by Paul van Riel/
Bimhuis; pp. 108–109 (Escape) by Jos Klijn, 2008/
www.klijn.info; pp. 110–113 (Jimmy Woo) courtesy
Jimmy Woo; pp. 114–115 (Little Buddha) p 115
bottom by Photo Dilani, all others by Erik Sawaya;
pp. 116–117 (Melkweg) by DigiDaan; pp. 118–119
(Papeneiland) by Hans Zaglitsch; pp. 120–123 (Sky
Lounge) by Matthew Shaw; pp. 124–125 (Noorderlicht) courtesy Noorderlicht; pp. 126–129 (Canvas
op de 7DE) pp. 126–127 and p 128 by Hans Zaglitsch,
all others by Elmer Driessen/Verveeld & Verwaand;
pp. 130–131 (Tonight) courtesy Hotel Arena; pp.
132–133 (Momo) p 133 top courtesy Momo, all
others by Rob ter Bekke; pp. 134–135 (Twenty
Third) courtesy Twenty Third

HIGHLIGHTS
pp. 138–141 (Amstel) by Hans Zaglitsch; pp. 142–143
(Begijnhof) by Hans Zaglitsch; pp. 144–145 (De Dam)
by Hans Zaglitsch; pp. 146–149 (De Jordaan) by
Hans Zaglitsch; pp. 150–151 (Hermitage) by Hans
Zaglitsch; pp. 152–153 (Leidseplein and Rembrandtplein) by Hans Zaglitsch; pp. 154–155 (Waterlooplein)
by Hans Zaglitsch; pp. 156–159 (Stadseilanden) by
Hans Zaglitsch; pp. 160–161 (Red Light District) by
Hans Zaglitsch; pp. 162–163 (Herengracht and Keizersgracht) by Hans Zaglitsch; pp. 164–165 (Museum
van Loon) by Hans Zaglitsch; pp. 166–169 (Prinsengracht) by Hans Zaglitsch; pp. 170–171 (Museum
Het Rembrandthuis) courtesy Museum Het Rembrandthuis; pp. 172–173 (De Pijp) by Hans Zaglitsch;
pp. 174–175 (Van-Gogh-Museum) p 174 top by Luuk
Kramer, p 174 bottom by Vincent van Gogh Found-
ation, p 175 by Jannes Linders/ all images courtesy
Van Gogh Museum; pp. 176–177 (Vondelpark)
by Hans Zaglitsch; p 190 (bicyles) by Hans Zaglitsch

COOL
CITIES
LIFESTYLE

Pocket-size Book
www.cool-cities.com

ISBN 978-3-8327-9490-3

ISBN 978-3-8327-9495-8

ISBN 978-3-8327-9484-2

ISBN 978-3-8327-9497-2

ISBN 978-3-8327-9595-5

ISBN 978-3-8327-9488-0

ISBN 978-3-8327-9496-5

ISBN 978-3-8327-9493-4

ISBN 978-3-8327-9489-7

ISBN 978-3-8327-9491-0

COOL
CITIES
ART ARCHITECTURE DESIGN

ISBN 978-3-8327-9435-4

ISBN 978-3-8327-9433-0

ISBN 978-3-8327-9463-7

ISBN 978-3-8327-9464-4

ISBN 978-3-8327-9501-6

ISBN 978-3-8327-9465-1

ISBN 978-3-8327-9502-3

ISBN 978-3-8327-9499-6

ISBN 978-3-8327-9434-7

COOL
CITIES

A NEW GENERATION
of multimedia lifestyle travel guides featuring the hippest, most fashionable hotels, shops, dining spots, galleries, and more for cosmopolitan travelers.

VISUAL
Discover the city with tons of brilliant photos and videos.

APP FEATURES
Search by categories, districts, or geolocator; get directions or create your own tour.

BARCELONA
SHANGHAI
TOKYO
SINGAPORE
BEIJING
VIENNA
PARIS
SYDNEY
HONG KONG
MUNICH
ZURICH
NEW YORK
SAO PAULO
AMSTERDAM
MIAMI
FRANKFURT
HAMBURG

ROME
EMIRATES
CHICAGO
MILAN
BERLIN

© 2012 Idea & concept by Martin Nicholas Kunz, Lizzy Courage Berlin
Selected and edited by Martin N. Kunz, Hans Zaglitsch
Introduction and location texts by Linda O'Bryan
Editorial Management: Miriam Bischoff
Photo Editor: David Burghardt
Copy Editor: Claudia Jürgens, Berlin
Layout and pre-press: Christin Steirat
Imaging: Tridix, Berlin
Translations: Heather Bock, Romina Russo

© 2012 teNeues Verlag GmbH + Co. KG, Kempen

teNeues Verlag GmbH + Co. KG
Am Selder 37, 47906 Kempen // Germany
Phone: +49 (0)2152 916-0, Fax: +49 (0)2152 916-111
e-mail: books@teneues.de

Press department: Andrea Rehn
Phone: +49 (0)2152 916-202 // e-mail: arehn@teneues.de

teNeues Digital Media GmbH
Kohlfurter Straße 41–43, 10999 Berlin // Germany
Phone: +49 (0)30700 77 65-0

teNeues Publishing Company
7 West 18th Street, New York, NY 10011 // USA
Phone: +1 212 627 9090, Fax: +1 212 627 9511

teNeues Publishing UK Ltd.
21 Marlowe Court, Lymer Avenue, London SE19 1LP // UK
Phone: +44 (0)20 8670 7522, Fax: +44 (0)20 8670 7523

teNeues France S.A.R.L.
39, rue des Billets, 18250 Henrichemont // France
Phone: +33 (0)2 4826 9348, Fax: +33 (0)1 7072 3482

www.teneues.com

Bibliographic information published by the Deutsche Nationalbibliothek.
The Deutsche Nationalbibliothek lists this publication in the
Deutsche Nationalbibliografie; detailed bibliographic data are
available in the Internet at http://dnb.d-nb.de.

v 1.0
Printed in the Czech Republic
ISBN: 978-3-8327-9627-3